The Literary Speech Act

THE LITERARY SPEECH ACT

Don Juan with J. L. Austin, or

Seduction in Two Languages

SHOSHANA FELMAN

TRANSLATED BY

Catherine Porter

Cornell University Press

ITHACA, NEW YORK

Originally published in French under the title *Le Scandale du corps parlant*, © Editions du Seuil, 1980.

Translation copyright © 1983 by Cornell University Press

First published 1983 by Cornell University Press.

International Standard Book Number 0-8014-1458-X
Library of Congress Catalog Card Number 83-45144
Printed in the United States of America
Librarians: Library of Congress cataloging information appears on the last page of the book.

The paper in this book is acid-free and meets the guidelines for permanence and durability of the Committee on Production Guidelines for Book Longevity of the Council on Library Resources.

Contents

Contents

Preface:
The Promising Animal

How am I to promise as if there were still in me
something left of my own?

                    —Claudel, *The Satin Slipper*

To breed an animal with the right to make promises—is not this the paradoxical problem nature has
set itself with regard to man? And is it not man's true
problem?
                    —Nietzsche, *Genealogy of Morals*

If promising can in some way, as Nietzsche suggests, define the problematics of the human, if it can *situate* what
makes for *problems* in man, it is not surprising that promising should have come recently to occupy center stage in
linguistic and philosophical theory. Current research on the
performative[1] is very often organized around promising,
which is taken as the exemplary model of speech acts in
general. "I shall take promising as my initial quarry," writes
John Searle, for one, "because as illocutionary acts go, it is
fairly formal and well articulated; like a mountainous terrain, it exhibits its geographical features starkly. But we
shall see that it has more than local interest, and many of

[1]Besides the works of J. L. Austin, which I shall examine in some detail
further on, and the work of Searle mentioned in the following note, see also
R. M. Hare, "The Promising Game," in *Revue internationale de philosophie,* 18 (1964), 398–412; Jonathan Harrison, "Knowing and Promising," in
Mind, 71 (Oct. 1962); John R. Searle, "How to Derive 'Ought' from 'Is'," in
Philosophical Review, 73 (1964); Jerome B. Schneewind, "A Note on Promising," in *Philosophical Studies,* 17 (April 1966).

the lessons to be learned from it are of general application."[2] Owing to their stark contours, these mountainlike promises doubtless cast shadows in one direction or another, shadows that, paradoxically, may be as illuminating as the light of the performative itself. The exploration of these shadows is the task this book will undertake.

What, then, is a promise? What exactly are we doing when we say "I promise," and what are the consequences? All these questions are addressed by the logicians of language who deal with the performative. But here I should like to displace the findings of linguistic and logical analysis somewhat, in order to bring to bear upon them the Nietzschean question: In what way does a promise constitute a paradox, a problem? In what way is the very logic of promising a sign of a fundamental contradiction which is precisely the contradiction of the human? These latter questions, although they are implied by the performative, do not lie strictly within the domain of formal linguistic research; they emerge again, on the other hand, at the heart of a famous literary myth which raises the problem of the performative in a spectacular way, the myth of Don Juan.[3]

Don Juan in fact lavishes promises right and left, and breaks them repeatedly. "I *repeat the promise* I made you," he says to Charlotte (II, ii), but he is soon whispering to Mathurine: "I *bet* she's going to tell you that I *promised* to marry her"; and then, to Charlotte, "*Let's bet* she'll argue that I *gave her my word* I'd marry her." "He saw me . . . and *promised* to marry me," Charlotte maintains. But Mathurine protests: "It's me and not you he *promised* to marry." "Sir, did you *promise* to marry her?" asks Charlotte. And

[2] John R. Searle, *Speech Acts: An Essay in the Philosophy of Language* (Cambridge: Cambridge University Press, 1969), p. 54.

[3] The two principal references to the Don Juan myth in this book will be, first, Molière's *Don Juan* and, second, the *Don Giovanni* of Mozart and Da Ponte. As a general rule, all quotations followed by roman numerals (indicating act and scene) refer to Molière's play. For the French text, see Molière, *Oeuvres complètes* (Paris: Seuil, Coll. "L'Intégrale," 1962); for a complete English translation, see Wallace Fowlie, *Don Juan or the Statue at the Banquet* (Great Neck, N.Y.: Barron's Educational Series, 1964). All passages quoted here have been translated directly from the French.

Mathurine: "Is it true, sir, that you *promised* to be her husband?" And Don Juan replies: "Both of you claim I *promised* to marry you. . . . Shouldn't the girl I really *promised* be able to ignore what the other one says? What does she have to worry about, *provided that I keep my promise?* All the discussion in the world won't help matters. We have to act, not talk; actions speak louder than words" (II, iv). Don Juan obviously abuses the institution of promising. But what does this abuse signify about promising itself? The scandal of seduction seems to be fundamentally tied to the scandal of the broken promise. *Don Juan* is the myth of scandal precisely to the extent that it is the myth of violation: the violation not of women but of promises made to them; in particular, promises of marriage. The question that this book will raise is thus twofold: how does research on the performative shed light on the myth of Don Juan? but also, on the other hand, what light does the Don Juan myth shed on performative theory? Our reading of Molière's *Don Juan* in the light of the writings of J. L. Austin and Emile Benveniste will be followed—paralleled and exceeded—by a reading of the Austin/Benveniste polemic, itself in turn illuminated by the text of *Don Juan*. On the basis, then, of a triple reading—of a literary text, a linguistic text, and a philosophical text—I want to undertake a meditation on promising, in such a way that the place of the literary will become the meeting and testing ground of the linguistic and the philosophical, the place where linguistics and philosophy are interrogated but also where they are pushed beyond their disciplinary limits.

Now it is at the very moment of this overreaching or outdistancing that the literary, producing analytic effects and thus giving rise to the necessity—and the possibility— of a theoretical articulation between psychoanalysis and the performative (an articulation that brings both theories out into a new light), opens onto an irreducible *scandal:* the scandal (which is at once theoretical and empirical, historical) of the incongruous but indissoluble relation between language and the body; the scandal of the *seduction* of the human body insofar as it speaks—the scandal of the promise of love insofar as this promise is *par excellence* the promise that cannot be kept; the scandal of the promising animal insofar as what he promises is precisely the *untenable.*

To write the scandal of the speaking body, to speak the scandal of seduction, that which grounds, in my view, the literary order, the theoretical order, and the historical order in turn, to do this here will thus mean attempting to articulate something at the crossroads of several disciplines (the point where psychoanalysis, linguistics, philosophy, literature, etc., meet and fail to meet . . .) and at the crossroads of language (where English and French, or theoretical language and literary, rhetorical language, meet and fail to meet); attempting to articulate not so much what is *said* or could be said but what is happening, taking effect, producing acts, what is being *done* or could be done between speaking bodies, between languages, between knowledge and pleasure.

To speak an act: can this be done? Is it possible to speak seduction—the always scandalous intervention of love in theory, of pleasure in knowledge?

Perhaps I have only spoken the seduction exercised on me by certain texts, certain theories, certain languages; perhaps I have in turn, in this book, only perpetrated scandal, only articulated my own promise. Perhaps I have spoken here only the unknown of my own pleasure. May readers, in any case, find their own pleasure here—that is my hope.

I

Between Linguistics and
Philosophy of Language:
Theories of Promise,
Promises of Theory

The Reflections of J. L. Austin:
Between Truth and Felicity

The English philosopher J. L. Austin, who initiated speech-act research and introduced the term "performative," began by demystifying—in a thoroughly Nietzschean manner, moreover—the illusion upheld by the history of philosophy according to which the only thing at stake in language is its "truth" or "falsity."[1] If the attribute of truth or falsehood is indeed applicable to the category of utterances that Austin labels *constatives,* that is, to descriptive utterances, to sentences that set forth *statements* of fact, that report a state of affairs, true or false, this attribute is inapplicable, on the other hand, to another category of utterances, henceforth christened *performatives:* expressions whose function is not to inform or to describe, but to carry out a "performance," to accomplish an *act* through the very process of their enunciation. The first example chosen (and this choice will turn out to be significant for us later on) to

[1] *How to Do Things with Words,* 2d ed., J. O. Urmson and Marina Sbisà (Cambridge: Harvard University Press, 1975), pp. 101–102. This work will be identified henceforth by the abbreviation *HT.*

illustrate the performative is the linguistic act by means of which a marriage is performed: according to Austin, when I respond in the affirmative to the ritual and legal question posed during a marriage ceremony—"Do you take this woman to be your lawful wedded wife?" I am not *describing* what I am doing, I am *acting*; by saying "I do," I am accomplishing the marriage. Likewise, when I say "I promise," "I swear," "I apologize," I am not describing my act but accomplishing it; by speaking, by pronouncing these words, I produce the *event* that they designate: the very act of promising, swearing, apologizing, and so forth. And since, in this case, to speak is to act, performative utterances, inasmuch as they produce actions, and constitute operations, cannot be logically true or false, but only successful or unsuccessful, "felicitous" or "infelicitous." Thus in place of the truth/falsity criterion, essential to constative language, Austin substitutes in the case of performative language the criterion of felicity as opposed to infelicity, that is, the success or failure of the act or operation in question.

After listing the ways in which the performative can fail,[2] Austin sets out to find a specifically linguistic criterion that would make it possible to identify and recognize the per-

---

[2]*HT*, Lecture II. Failures are divided into two major categories: "misfires" and "abuses." Misfires result when the intended outcome of the performative utterance does not occur, *is not carried out*, owing to inappropriate circumstances: for example, because the conventional procedures to which performatives are always attached through their more or less ritual accomplishment were not respected, or were not in order. If I say, for example, "I take this woman as my lawful wedded wife" outside of the ritual ceremony, or when I am already married, the marriage is of course null and void, the act is not accomplished; it succumbs to the "infelicity" of failure; the performative utterance misfires. If on the other hand I say "I promise," but *without* the intention of keeping my promise, or in full knowledge that I will be unable to keep it, the performative act of promising is infelicitous because of an "abuse," not because of a misfire—it is not null and void. Indeed, whether or not I am sincere, when I utter the words "I promise" I in fact *carry out* the *act* of promising; the act succeeds, it is executed; but it may be executed in bad faith: by executing the act of promising, in such a case, I deceive my interlocutor. Although the act is "successful," then, it entails a form of failure; it is infelicitous because of my abuse.

formative, and would thus formally consolidate the opposition established between performative and constative. It is here that the philosopher's reflections, reaching an impasse, change direction. For although linguistic criteria that might formalize the distinction do exist, they prove to be neither exhaustive nor at all absolute. The principal grammatical criterion is the asymmetry that occurs, in certain verbs (henceforth recognized as "performative verbs"), between the first person of the present indicative, active voice, and the other persons and tenses of the verb: whereas the first person, by uttering the verb in the present tense, effectively carries out the designated act ("I *promise*," "I *swear*," I *guarantee*," "I *name* this ship the *Liberty*," "I *call* the meeting *to order*"—said by the presiding officer), all other forms of the verb are descriptions, not acts; they only state or report the event "I promised," "he swears," "he names this ship . . . ," "she called the meeting to order," and so on). But this criterion is insufficient, for we find other expressions that do not include an explicit performative verb and yet still belong to the category of the performative because they too accomplish an action and lie outside the reach of the truth/falsity criterion. The imperative, for example, "Go away!", may be seen as an ellipsis of the performative "I *order* you to leave." Or the sign "Beware of the dog" can be translated by the performative "I warn you that this dog bites." Thus we have to distinguish between explicit and implicit performatives. But as soon as we acknowledge the existence of implicit performatives, it is difficult to find any sentence that would not fall into this category. For even constative utterances might imply the ellipsis of "I note," "I affirm," "I declare": these expressions too, in the last analysis, do no more than carry out linguistic *acts* which are neither true nor false but which on the other hand may be successful or unsuccessful, felicitous or infelicitous. "What we need to do for the case of stating, and by the same token describing and reporting," Austin writes, "is to take them a bit off their pedestal, to realize that they are speech-acts no less than all these other speech-acts that we have been mentioning and talking about as performative."[3] "If, then, we loosen up our ideas of truth and falsity we shall see that statements, when assessed in relation to the facts, are not so very different after all from pieces of advice, warnings, verdicts, and so on" (*PP*, p. 251).

The original distinction between performative and constative is thus weakened, and indeed dislocated. What is needed in its place, Austin concludes, is a general theory of speech acts as such.

Austin provides this general theory in his doctrine of illocution. Encompassing and broadening the concept of the performative, the "illocutionary act" is the speech performance examined with reference to the *context* of the interlocution, to the concrete and conventional discursive situation in which speech acquires, above and beyond its meaning, a certain force of utterance (the force of warning, commitment, plea, command, and so on). In his analysis of language, Austin thus distinguishes *meaning* and *force*: the two almost always coexist in the production of speech. He labels the production of *meaning* a "*locutionary* act," and opposes this to the power plays of the "*illocutionary* act." These two types of speech acts are both contrasted, in turn, with a third type, called "*perlocutionary* acts," consisting in the production of *effects* on the *interlocutor* (surprising, convincing, deceiving, misleading, and so on). Thus "he said to me: 'Shoot her!' meaning by 'shoot' shoot and referring by 'her' to *her*" is a locutionary act; "he urged (or advised, ordered, &c.) me to shoot her" is an illocutionary act; "he persuaded me to shoot her" or "he got me to (or made me, &c.) shoot her" is a perlocutionary act (*HT*, pp. 101–102).

The performative as such thus takes its place within a general doctrine of illocution and of enunciatory forces, which Austin divides into five categories:

---

[3]J. L. Austin, "Performative Utterances," in *Philosophical Papers*, ed. J. O. Urmson and G. L. Warnock (Oxford and New York: Oxford University Press, 1979, 3d ed.), pp. 249–250. This collection of Austin's articles will be identified henceforth by the abbreviation *PP*.

(1). The category of verdicts (*verdictives*): speech acts that constitute the exercise of judgment (condemning, acquitting, estimating, evaluating, etc.).

(2). The category of orders (*exercitives*): speech acts that constitute assertions of authority or the exercise of power (commanding, giving an order, naming, advising, pardoning, etc.).

(3). The category of commitments (*commissives*): speech acts that consist in the assumption of an engagement with respect to a future action (promising, contracting, espousing, enrolling, swearing, betting, etc.).

(4). The category of behaviors (*behabitives*): speech acts linked to a social posture (congratulating, apologizing, greeting, etc.).

(5). The category of expositions (*expositives*): speech acts that consist in a discursive clarification (affirming, denying, questioning, asking, remarking, etc.) (*HT*, pp. 151–163).

Emile Benveniste's Modifications: Felicity and Legitimacy

Recognizing the importance of the category of the performative for linguistics itself, Emile Benveniste opposes the broadening of this category, and consequently dissociates himself from the general doctrine of illocutionary acts. "We see no reason for abandoning the distinction between the performative and the constative. We believe it justified and necessary. . . . If one does not hold to precise criteria of a formal and linguistic order, and particularly if one is not careful to distinguish between sense and reference, one endangers the very object of analytic philosophy; the specificity of language in the circumstances in which the linguistic forms one chooses to study are valid."[4]

[4]Emile Benveniste, *Problems in General Linguistics*, trans. M. E. Meek

Setting out to provide a more precise description of the performative from a strictly linguistic standpoint, Benveniste's critical reassessment of Austin's theory turns out to include—when we attempt to summarize it analytically—three subtractions (exclusions) and four additions (specifications, definitional elements).

The three subtractions, or exclusionary moves, are presented in the form of secondary methodological notes, but in fact they constitute three analytical principles:

(1). *The exclusion of the general theory of illocutionary forces:* this serves to safeguard the formal purity of the constative/performative opposition.

(2). *The exclusion of the theory of failures or infelicities ("unhappinesses") of the performative:* "We have taken . . . only the most salient points of the line of reasoning and those arguments in the demonstration which touched upon facts which are properly linguistic. Thus we [shall not] examine the considerations of the logical 'unhappinesses' which can overtake and render inoperative either type of utterance" (Benveniste, p. 234). Later on, discussing the "unhappiness" of an unrealized performative, Benveniste explains that such an utterance simply does not exist as a performative; thus it is excluded from the category: "Anybody can shout in the public square, 'I decree a general mobilization,' and as it cannot be an *act** because the requisite authority is lacking, such an utterance is no more than *words**; it reduces itself to futile clamor, childishness, or lunacy. *A performative utterance that is not an act does not exist"* (p. 236; *Benveniste's emphasis[5]).

(3). *The exclusion of clichés* from the category of the performative. "We are not at all certain that the locutions cited

---

(Coral Gables, Fla.: University of Miami Press, 1971), chapter 22: "Analytical Philosophy and Language," p. 238. All quotations from Benveniste are taken from this study, to which I shall return several times in the course of this book.

[5]As a general rule and unless otherwise indicated, passages italicized in quoted material are those I myself have chosen to emphasize. Passages that are emphasized by the authors themselves will be identified parenthetically.

above (*I welcome you; I apologize; I advise you to do it*) can be given as conclusive proof for the notion of the performative. At least, they are not proof today because social life has made them so trite. Since they have fallen to the rank of simple formulae, they must be brought back to their original sense in order for them to regain their performative function" (Benveniste, p. 234). Thus it is preferable to avoid studying performative utterances that have fallen into disuse, those whose situational contexts no longer exist, and instead to choose "performatives in full use" (p. 234).

Having thus excluded from the category of the performative all clichés, failures, and those performatives that the general doctrine of illocutionary acts treats as implicit or pervasive, Benveniste in turn adds four supplemental specifications to the definition of the performative:

(1). *Performative utterances are always acts of authority;* of legitimate authority, to be sure. "A performative utterance . . . has existence only as an act of authority. Now, acts of authority are first and always utterances made by those to whom the right to utter them belongs. This condition of validity, related to the person making the utterance and to the circumstances of the utterance, must always be considered met when one deals with the performative. The criterion is here and not in the choice of verbs" (p. 236).

(2). Insofar as it is an act, *the performative utterance has the property of being unique.* "It cannot be produced except in special circumstances, at one and only one time, at a definite date and place. . . . Being an individual and historical act, a performative utterance *cannot be repeated.* Each reproduction is a new act performed by someone who is qualified. Otherwise, the reproduction of the performative utterance by someone else necessarily transforms it into a constative utterance" (p. 236).

(3). *The performative is defined by a singular property, that of being self-referential,* of referring to a reality that it constitutes itself. It is at once a linguistic manifestation and a real fact. "The act is thus identical with the utterance of the act. The signified is identical to the referent. . . . The utterance that takes itself as a referent is indeed self-referential" (p. 236).

(4). *The performative utterance is an act of naming* the act performed and its agent. "An utterance is performative in that it denominates the act performed. . . . Hence a performative utterance must name the spoken performance as well as its performer. . . . The utterance *is* the act; the one who pronounces it performs the act in denominating it" (p. 237; Benveniste's emphasis).

By adding these four criteria, these four formal specifications, to performative theory, Benveniste reaffirms and reinstates the decisive opposition between constative and performative.

II

The Perversion of Promising:
Don Juan and
Literary Performance

Fundamentally, the realm of eroticism is the realm
of violence, the realm of violation.
—Bataille, *L'Erotisme*

What is strangest of all is the popular conviction that
a lover, and none but a lover, can forswear himself
with impunity—a lover's vow, they say, is no vow at
all.
—Plato, *The Symposium*

The Don Juan Conflict and
Illocutionary Forces of Commitment

With the exception of the end, that is, of the supernatural conclusion, the action of Molière's *Don Juan* is made up entirely of performative events: language acts of which the *forces* of utterance could be appropriately described in terms of the five illocutionary classes Austin distinguishes:

(1). Verdictive performatives, or exercises of judgment (accomplished throughout the play by Don Juan's antagonists);

(2). Imperative performatives, or exercises of power (Don Juan to Sganarelle);

(3). Promissory performatives, or exercises of the act of promising (Don Juan to the women);

(4). Behavioral performatives and performatives of social ritual, exercises of politeness (Don Juan to Monsieur Dimanche);

(5). Performatives of exposition and argumentation (Sganarelle to Don Juan).

If the illocutionary force deployed by Don Juan is above all that of promising, the one that his antagonists and pursuers use is, on the other hand, a force of threat or warning. Now threats, too, constitute a sort of negative promise:[1] if promising consists in committing oneself to do something *for* someone, then, similarly, threatening consists in committing oneself to do something *against* someone. Although the *meaning* of the promise (love and marriage) is of course different from that of the threat (revenge and punishment), the *force* behind both is the same. The conflict that opposes Don Juan to his pursuers thus opposes a promise to a threat—to a negative promise resulting from Don Juan's failure to keep a positive promise, but also a positive promise not to fail to punish the failure to keep that promise. *Don Juan* is thus indeed a play about promising. But the paradox of the promise (perhaps the paradox Nietzsche was referring to) is revealed here in the fact that the promise not only *gives rise* to the conflict, but *structures* it: the agonistic tension of the play in fact opposes, fundamentally and paradoxically, antagonistic forces of the *same type*—forces that, on both sides, belong to the *category of commitment*. It is within the illocutionary category of commitment that both the division and the opposition are produced. If the play is thus "about" promising, it seems, in a certain way, to dramatize within the promise a sort of internal cleavage, an inherent dehiscence.

Opposing Views of Language

If the essential similarity of the opposing forces eludes the protagonists, however, it is because the various individuals who perform acts of commitment have differing concepts of language. What is really at stake in the play—the real con-

---

[1] See John R. Searle, *Speech Acts: An Essay in the Philosophy of Language* (Cambridge: Cambridge University Press, 1969), p. 58, and Jerrold J. Katz, *Propositional Structure and Illocutionary Force*, (New York: Crowell, 1977), p. 190: "Threats promise harm to people."

flict—is, in fact, the opposition between two views of language, one that is cognitive, or constative, and another that is performative. According the cognitive view, which characterizes Don Juan's antagonists and victims, language is an instrument for transmitting *truth*, that is, an instrument of knowledge, a means of *knowing* reality. Truth is a relation of perfect congruence between an utterance and its referent, and, in a general way, between language and the reality it represents. If it is not given to man to know truth in its totality, such absolute knowledge exists nonetheless in the word of God, in whose omniscience, indeed, language originates. Thus incarnating the authority of truth, God, or the "voice of Heaven" (that is, the fact that God speaks), underwrites the authority of language as a cognitive instrument. In this view, the sole function reserved for language is the *constative* function: what is at stake in an utterance is its correspondence—or lack of correspondence—to its real referent, that is, its truth or falsity.

Indeed, determining the degree of truth or falsity of Don Juan's statements seems to be the chief preoccupation of the characters in the play. "I don't know if you're telling the truth or not," says Charlotte (II, ii). "Is what you say really true?" Don Louis asks (V, i). And the two women insist:

> CHARLOTTE: No, no, we have to know the truth.
> MATHURINE: We have to settle this. [II, iv]

This is how the question of knowing is confused with the question of judging; the illocutionary act of judgment is experienced as a pure constative or cognitive effort.

However this may be, Don Juan does not share such a view of language. Saying, for him, is in no case tantamount to knowing, but rather to *doing: acting* on the interlocutor, modifying the situation and the interplay of forces within it. Language, for Don Juan, is performative and not informative; it is a field of enjoyment, not of knowledge. As such, it cannot be qualified as true or false, but rather quite specifically as *felicitous* or *infelicitous*, successful or unsuccessful.

Linguistic Felicity

If we consider the play in terms of success or failure, it is no doubt significant that Don Juan's spectacular erotic success is accomplished by linguistic means alone. When Don Juan decides for once to risk "performances" other than those of speech and to use physical force to carry his lady love off to sea, he experiences failure, "infelicity," a ship-wreck:

> We've *missed our chance,* Sganarelle; that unexpected storm has upset our plan as well as our boat. But the peasant girl I've just left makes up for this *misfortune* . . . and wipes out the memory of our *failure.* [II, ii]

On the other hand, Don Juan cannot *fail* (*misfire*) when he sets out to get a woman *by speaking.* The other side of the "misfire," the myth of Don Juan's irresistible seduction, dramatizes nothing other than the success of language, the felicity of the speech act.

⌈To seduce is to produce felicitous language.⌋Now for Don Juan, felicity itself is nothing other than having "no more to say": "It is extremely sweet to reduce a young beauty's heart to submission, through a hundred flatteries . . . But once you are master, there is *no more to say,* nor anything left to wish for; the best part of the passion is spent" (I, ii).

The desire of a Don Juan is thus at once desire for desire and desire for language; a desire that desires *itself* and that desires its own language. Speech is the true realm of eroti-cism, and not simply a means of access to this realm. To seduce is to produce language that enjoys, language that takes pleasure in having "no more to say." To seduce is thus to prolong, within desiring speech, the pleasure-taking per-formance of the very production of that speech.

The Donjuanian act of seduction in this way makes con-crete the relation, and the problem of the relation, among the three meanings of the word "act," three meanings that are homologous, moreover, with the three connotations of the word *performance* in English: the erotic connotation, the theatrical connotation, and the linguistic connotation. The question of man's eroticism is raised, through the Don Juan myth, as the question of the relation of the erotic and the linguistic on the stage of the speaking body, where fate is played out as that which, of this speaking body, *makes an act*. The Don Juan myth, in other words, dramatizes the notion of human action as the question of the relation between sexual act and speech act, between speech act and theatrical act. As such, this myth proposes itself as a mythical question to speech-act theory: what is speech, when it performs? What are acts, when language is involved? Why is the erotic success of a Don Juan necessarily bound up with linguistic "felicity"? Why does linguistic felicity appear, moreover, as the other side of the coin of the "infelicity" of a misfire? Since misfires, missed chances, are paired in Molière's play with broken promises, does this mean that to succeed erotically would be in some way, necessarily, to succeed at failing? What is the function of failure in eroticism, and in human action in general?

The Rhetoric of Seduction

Feelings are always reciprocal.

—Lacan

The world functions only through misunderstanding. It is through universal misunderstanding that everyone agrees. For if by misfortune people understood one another, they could never agree.

—Baudelaire, "My Heart Laid Bare"

If it is true, as Jean Rousset writes, that "Molière's Don Juan appears to be such a skillful seducer only because of his discourse—because he has turned himself meanwhile into a theoretician of Donjuanism,"[2] we still have to specify that Don Juan discourses only while making of discourse itself an *act*, and that his "theory of Donjuanism" could be read, in a certain way, as a speech-act theory.

The rhetoric of seduction consists, in fact, almost exclusively in the deployment of speech acts: Donjuanian debauchery is in reality above all a debauchery of explicit performatives—commissive performatives which are used, moreover, to seduce men just as much as women. Such performatives as these serve to seduce Elvira's brother Don Carlos: "I am a friend of Don Juan. . . . *I give my word* to make him do you justice . . . *I promise* to have him show up wherever you like, whenever you like. . . . *I answer for him* as for myself" (III, iii). Such performatives, too, seduce Monsieur Dimanche: "I am your servant, and moreover, I am in your debt. . . . Once again *I beg you to* believe that I am at your disposition; there is nothing in the world that I wouldn't do for you" (IV, iii). And those that seduce the women: "I call on this man here to *bear witness to what I am saying to you . . . I repeat* once again *the promise that I am making to you.* . . . Do you want me to swear fearful oaths? May Heaven . . . (II, ii); "*I bet* she's going to tell you that I promised to marry her. . . . *Let's bet* she'll argue that I gave her my word I'd marry her" (II, iv); "*I beg you* to remember what I said when I gave you my word" (II, v).

The rhetoric of seduction may in this way be summarized by the performative utterance *par excellence: "I promise,"* an utterance in which all the *force* of Don Juan's discourse is subsumed, and which is opposed, on the other hand, to the *meaning* of the discourse of the other characters in the play, a discourse that, for its part, is better summed up by Charlotte's demand—the constative demand *par excellence:* "We have to know the truth" (III, iii). The dialogue between

---

[2]"Don Juan et le baroque," in *Diogène*, 4 (1956), and in *Obliques* 4 (1974), *Don Juan: Analyse d'un mythe,* vol. I, p. 87. See also Jean Rousset, *Le Mythe de Don Juan* (Paris: Armand Colin, 1978).

Don Juan and the others is thus a dialogue between two orders that, in reality, do not communicate: the order of the act and the order of meaning, the register of pleasure and the register of knowledge. When he replies "I promise" to "we have to know the truth," the seducer's strategy is paradoxically to create, in a linguistic space that he himself controls, a *dialogue of the deaf*. For, by committing speech acts, Don Juan literally escapes the hold of truth. Although he has no intention whatsoever of keeping his promises, the seducer, strictly speaking, does not lie, since he is doing no more than playing on the self-referential property of these performative utterances, and is effectively accomplishing the speech acts that he is naming. The trap of seduction thus consists in producing a *referential illusion* through an utterance that is by its very nature *self-referential:* the illusion of a real or extralinguistic act of commitment created by an utterance that refers only to itself.

Just as seductive discourse exploits the capacity of language to reflect itself, by means of the self-referentiality of performative verbs, it also exploits in parallel fashion the self-referentiality of the interlocutor's narcissistic desire, and his (or her) capacity to produce in turn a reflexive, specular illusion: the seducer holds out to women the narcissistic mirror of their own desire of themselves. Thus Don Juan says to Charlotte: "You are not *obliged* to me for what I say, you owe it entirely to your own beauty. . . . Your beauty is your *security*" [*votre beauté vous assure de tout*] (II, ii). It is significant that the constative description of the woman also includes a vocabulary of commitment; the verbs (*obliger, assurer*) are performative, but they are no longer in the first person present indicative, thus they are no longer in the category of effective language acts. The source of obligation is displaced here from the first to the second and third persons: "You are not *obliged* to me . . . your beauty is your security." The constative itself, in Don Juan's mouth, appears to be the *statement of a promise*, of a commitment undertaken. Whether constative or performative, seductive discourse commits and endebts; but since the debt is contracted here on the basis of narcissism, the two parties to the debt are the woman and her own self-image. "Your beauty is your security." The specular illusion of self-reference allows Don Juan to elude the status of referent. While the seducer appears to be committing himself, his strategy is to create a *reflexive, self-referential debt* that, as such, does not engage *him*. Thus Charlotte's seduction by Don Juan does not differ in essence from that of Monsieur Dimanche: "It's true, he pays me so many courtesies and compliments that I could never ask him for money" (IV, iii). The scandal of seduction thus consists in a skillful and lucid exploitation, by Don Juan, of the specular structure of the meaning and reflexive capacities of language.

Eroticism and Theology

Don Juan nevertheless poses a problem for those around him, and constitutes a scandal not only as seducer but also as atheist, iconoclast, unbeliever: "A madman, a dog, a devil, a Turk, a heretic who believes neither in Heaven nor in Hell . . . and treats all that we believe in as nonsense" (I, i). Is there a connection that articulates seduction and unbelief in some necessary fashion, and that thus accounts at the same time for the double scandal of Don Juan?

It seems to me in reality that unbelief, in the Don Juan myth, is only the logical consequence, even the theoretical implication, of the practice of seduction. Don Juan does not believe, because he *makes (others) believe.* He knows perfectly well that belief is only the effect of the reflection, the reflexivity that he exploits: even though he refers his interlocutors back to themselves, even though he profits from the self-referentiality of the explicit performance, he still succeeds in creating belief in his ontological commitment and in the objective reality of the specular illusions that he produces. The act of seduction is above all an inducer of belief.

> DON JUAN: There is nothing I wouldn't do for you.
> MONSIEUR DIMANCHE: Sir, you are too good to me.
> DON JUAN: I have only your interest at heart, *I beg you to believe me.*
> SGANARELLE: I *assure* you that his entire household would die for you. . . .
> MONSIEUR DIMANCHE: *I believe it.* [IV, iii]

> CHARLOTTE: . . . *I would like nothing better in the world than to believe you.* . . . Lord! I don't know if you're telling the truth or not, but you *make* people *believe* you. [II, ii]

Thus, for Don Juan, belief, which he manipulates in others, is always a performance of language, an illusory meaning-effect produced by a reflexive and self-referential signifier.

But, as we have said, whereas for Don Juan language—as a performative field of pleasure—is a fundamentally self-referential field, for the others language—as a constative field of knowledge—is referential, capable of transitive reference. Thus Don Juan's atheism is opposed to the others' religion as an atheistic, indeed a self-referential, concept of language is opposed to a theological, referential concept. Like eroticism, theology in the Don Juan myth is played out exclusively on the stage of language. Donjuanian unbelief is above all disbelief in the capacity of language to name a transitive truth.

The Promise of Marriage

The heretical act *par excellence* that emblematizes, in Don Juan's behavior, both the scandal of seduction and the scandal of unbelief is his repetitive violation of the institution of marriage.

SGANARELLE: It costs him nothing to get married; he doesn't need to use any other trap to catch his lady friends. He gets married all the time [he is a marrier at every hand]. [I, i]

SGANARELLE: But to see you getting married every month the way you do . . . playing like that with a sacred mystery. . . .
DON JUAN: Come now, this is between Heaven and myself, we'll sort it out together. [I, ii]

If the discourse of seduction is as such a discourse of promising, it is perhaps no accident that the Donjuanian promise is always a promise of marriage. What the Don Juan myth thus brings out is that a necessary link exists between the notion of the promise and that of marriage. The French language itself suggests this relationship, since the etymological meaning of the verb *épouser*, "to marry," is "to promise,"[3] and since, furthermore, the adjective forms *promis, promise* signify "engaged." This interaction of meaning between "promise" and "marriage" becomes all the more striking when we note that Austin in his definition of "commissives"—the category of illocutionary acts of commitment—specified two types of acts of commitment: on the other hand, promises proper, and, on the other hand, what he chooses, curiously, to call "espousals": "[commissives also include] rather vague things which we may call espousals, as for example, siding with" (*HT*, p. 152). Every commitment may thus be seen as the action of espousing something (or someone).[4] If every marriage is, of course, a promise, every promise is to a certain extent a promise of marriage—to the extent that every promise promises *constancy* above all, that is, promises consistency, continuity in time between the act of commitment and the future action. "Any speech act," says Austin, "[commits us] at least

[3]Cf. the English word "espouse," which derives from Middle English *espousen*, from Old French *espouser*, from Late Latin *sponsare*, from Latin *spondere*, to promise solemnly (*American Heritage Dictionary*, 1970).
[4]One of the meanings of the French word *épouser* is "to adapt oneself precisely to (a form, a movement)" (*Petit Robert*, 1967). Every commitment is thus based on the hope of a perfect symmetry, that of marriage itself.

to consistency" (*HT*, p. 154). Don Juan is of course only playing, through the multiplicity of his promises of marriage, with the *illusion* of constancy inherent in the promise, an illusion in which he scarcely believes himself. This is why he is, mythically speaking, the figure of Inconstancy, of Unfaithfulness.

Now if the French language, in parallel with the Don Juan myth, informs us about the inherent relation between promising and marriage, this same language has another surprise in store on the very subject of constancy. As if by chance, in etymological terms "constancy" is precisely what serves to define the constative! As Benveniste notes, "a *constatif* statement is indeed a statement of a *constat* (established fact). Although *constat* is etymologically the Latin present *constat* 'it is established,' French treats it like a substantive of the same series as *résultat* and thus attaches it to the family of the ancient verb *conster*, "to be established" (p. 309, n. 10). Thus it is no accident that, in the Don Juan myth, this very figure of Inconstancy is what subverts the constative. Like marriage, the constative too turns out to be a promise of constancy: a promise that meaning will last; a promise underwritten, from the standpoint of the other characters in the play, by the constancy of God himself, by the voice of Heaven—a promise that is in the last analysis only the promise of language to refer, to make sense, to ensure a meaning that will be lasting, constant, constative. Thus, when he invokes Heaven—"Do you want me to swear fearful oaths? May Heaven . . ." (ii, ii)—and appears to acknowledge [*constater*] his promise of marriage ("the promise I've made you" [ii, ii]),[5] Don Juan in fact does nothing but *promise the constative.*

Now it is Don Juan himself who does not believe in his own promises. Unbelieving, the mythical seducer refuses to be seduced by his own myth, refuses for his part to be seduced by language, to believe in the promise of meaning.

---

[5]See also ii, v: "I beg you to remember what I said when I gave you my word."

Theology and Arithmetic

> SGANARELLE: You have an unbelieving nature. . . . Is it possible that you don't believe in Heaven? . . . But you have to believe in *something*. What *do* you believe in?
> DON JUAN: I believe that two and two are four, Sganarelle, and that four and four are eight.
> SGANARELLE: What a fine belief . . . that is! So if I understand you correctly, your religion is arithmetic? [III, i]

What does this belief in numbers, in arithmetic, signify for Don Juan? How is arithmetic opposed to religion? What are the philosophical implications of the assertion: "I believe that two and two are four"?

I believe that 2 + 2 = 4

(1). I believe in Arithmos, in Numbers, in quantification (quantity as opposed to quality), in the art of calculating, in the properties of rational numbers.

(2). I believe in a truth that is obtained only from the reduction of the linguistic system of meaning; I believe in the arithmetic system insofar as it has, strictly speaking, no meaning, insofar as it is an entirely self-referential system, determined by its own axioms, and one that therefore depends neither upon language nor upon reality for its validity.

(3). I believe in the plus sign (+), that is, in the principle of addition. I accumulate women, I add up spouses; the catalogue of their names may be, as Sganarelle puts it, "a chapter that will last all day" (I, ii). I believe in enumeration insofar as it constitutes an infinite series not subject to summation.

(4). I believe in the equals sign (=), that is, in the principle of equivalence and in the principle of equality.

> DON JUAN: But what do I see here? One man attacked by three others? *The match is too uneven,* I can't allow such cowardice. [III, ii]

LA RAMÉE: Twelve men on horseback are looking for you. . . .
DON JUAN: . . . *Since it's not an even match*, I'll have to use some stratagem. . . . [II, v]

(5) Believing in the principle of equivalence, I believe necessarily in the principle of infinite substitutability:

DON JUAN (*spotting Charlotte*): Ah! ah! where does this other peasant girl come from, Sganarelle? Have you ever seen anything prettier? Don't you think . . . that *this one is as good as the other?* [II, ii]

(6). Believing in the principle of infinite substitutability ("this one is as good as the other"), I believe in cardinal numbers and not in ordinal numbers. The connection between the one and the many does not imply an ordered relation; there exists no privileged number, more determining than the others, to which the series would be subordinated.

It is true that Mathurine and Charlotte believe in ordered relations:

MATHURINE: The gentleman saw me *first.*
CHARLOTTE: If he saw you first, he saw me *second*, and he promised to marry me. [II, iv]

But Mathurine and Charlotte are both wrong: for Don Juan, what number by definition *excludes* is precisely the relation of order, the relation of hierarchy. If "two and two are four," one = one, that is, any "one" equals any other "one." Thus the Donjuanian belief in arithmetic is atheological in that it deconstructs, above all, the hierarchical value of the "first."

DON JUAN: What? You think we should commit ourselves to stay with the *first* object that takes our fancy? . . . the advantage of being met *first* shouldn't deprive the others of the just claims they all have on our hearts. [I, ii]

Genetic Reasoning, or the
Promise of Paternity

Life doubtless reproduces, God knows what and
why. But the response is in question only where
there is no relation to support the reproduction of
life.
—Lacan, "L'Etourdit"

What do you suppose is the use of a child without
any meaning?
—Lewis Carroll, *Through the Looking-Glass*

The Donjuanian deconstruction of the value of the
"first," of the principle of an ordinal series, inplies at the
same time a general deconstruction of the very concept of
beginning as a basis for identities. In this way Don Juan
subverts the principle of genetic reasoning and the institution of paternity.[6] "You are unworthy of your ancestors,"
Don Louis, his father, says to him: "This son, for whom I
wore out Heaven with my prayers, is the sorrow and tor-
ment of the very life whose joy and consolation I believed he
would be" (IV, iv). Paternity itself appears here as an act of
language (to wear out Heaven with one's prayers), and son-
ship as a promise of Heaven. Now Don Juan, in his role as
son as in that of lover, again makes concrete the figure of a
promise not kept—a subversion of the *belief* tied to the
promise of Heaven: "this son . . . is the sorrow . . . of the
very life whose joy . . . I *believed* he would be." The supreme act, that of begetting a son, fails to produce meaning;
the paternal performance fails to produce the constative:
"Alas, how little we know what we are doing," says Don
Louis (IV, iv). As a promise not kept, Don Juan emblematizes

[6]On the very rich—and highly suggestive—relationship between paternity and divinity depicted in the text of *Don Juan*, see Jacques Guichar-
naud, *Molière, une aventure théâtrale* (Paris: Gallimard, 1963).

the rupture and the gap between paternal consciousness and paternal performance, the discontinuity between intention and act: the lack of self-knowledge of the very act of production of meaning; the "infelicity" or failure of the Father in his role as constative, cognitive authority.

In what, more precisely, does it consist, that promise of paternity that Don Juan disappoints and whose abortion he incarnates? Don Louis makes reference to this promise: "We share in the glory of our ancestors *only to the extent that we try to resemble them,* and the renown of their actions that they shower on us requires that we *commit ourselves* to *follow the path that they have traced"* (IV, iv). Thus the promise of paternal meaning, the promise of the act of begetting itself, is that of a relation of consistency and of resemblance of son to father, of sign to its referent. The paternal promise is, in other words, a promise of metaphor: of metaphor as a basis for the principle of identity, that is, as the promise of a *proper meaning* and of a *proper name.* "What have you done in the world?", Don Louis asks Don Juan, "to be a gentleman? Do you think it's enough to *bear the name* . . . ? No, no, birth counts for nothing where there is no virtue. And we share in the glory of our ancestors only to the extent that we try to resemble them" (IV, iv).

Anaphora/Metaphor

Don Juan, however, deconstructs this paternal logic of identity, this promise of *metaphor,* by the very figure of his own life, which is that of the *anaphora,* of the act of beginning ceaselessly renewed through the repetition of promises not carried out, not kept. "It's no use committing myself, my love for one beautiful woman does not commit my soul to be unjust to the others. . . . Falling in love, after all, has an inexplicable charm, and the whole pleasure of love lies in change" (I, ii). From the beginning, the anaphora thus repeats only inconsistency or disconnectedness. Paradoxically, the failure to carry out the promise makes it possible to begin it again: it is because the amorous promise is not kept that it can be renewed. Now if the figure of a new beginning is at the same time that of a lack of accomplishment, this is so insofar as the new beginning in Don Juan's consciousness is itself a denegation of the end, that is, a denial of death. Thus Don Juan explains his infidelity to Elvira and, more generally, the reason for his unmet commitments, the cause of his promise-breaking. "It's a fine thing to boast of the false honor of *being faithful*, of *burying oneself forever* in a passion and *being dead* from youth onward to all other beauties. . . . Falling in love, after all, has an inexplicable charm . . ." (I, ii). In the Donjuanian perspective, faithfulness is tantamount to an acceptance of the end, of *death*, whereas "falling in love" [*les inclinations naissantes*] constitutes precisely a new *birth*. The passage from one woman to another, from Elvira to the fiancée whom Don Juan proposes to carry off by sea, is thus explained as the necessity of transcending death by the experience of rebirth. Now the same structure is present, symbolically, in the shift to the following woman, the abandonment of the fiancée at sea and the flirtation begun with Mathurine, since this latter switch is occasioned by a shipwreck during which Don Juan barely escapes death. Saved by Pierrot, Don Juan emerges from the water *naked* as the day he was born: "Is he still all naked at your house?" asks Charlotte (II, i). Just as in a baptism, Don Juan's nudity as he emerges from the water dramatizes a symbolic rebirth, engendered by the very death that it denies:

> DON JUAN: We've *missed our chance*, Sganarelle; that unexpected storm has upset our plan as well as our boat. But the peasant girl I've just left makes up for this *misfortune*. . . .
> SGANARELLE: Sir . . . We've barely *escaped with our lives* and instead of thanking Heaven for it . . . , you're working again at getting it angry with us . . . with your love affairs. [II, ii]

Death's Crossings, or the Paradox of the Limit

Sleep and Death, you promise nothing, you keep everything.
                                    —Kierkegaard, *Either/Or*

If Donjuanian eroticism presents itself, structurally and symbolically, as a relation with death, the passage from one woman to another, that is, the promise-breaking itself, turns out to be a breach in memory (a breach in the memory of desire) to the extent that it constitutes an *act of forgetting* death. For Nietzsche, "oblivion is not merely a *vis inertiae,* as is often claimed, but an active screening device,"[7] and, in the strictest sense, a positive one:

> If happiness and the chase for new happiness keep alive in any sense the will to live, no philosophy has perhaps more truth than the cynic's. . . . In the smallest and greatest happiness there is always one thing that makes it happiness: the power of forgetting, or, in more learned phrase, the capacity of feeling "unhistorically" throughout its duration. . . . Forgetfulness is a property of all action.[8]

If life is conditioned by the capacity to forget, and if, on the other hand, promise-breaking in Molière's play is structurally an act of forgetting death, of consigning it to oblivion, then in the myth of seduction and of the shift from one woman to another we may read the affirmation of life as the ceaseless repetition of the crossing of death-lines: like a movement which, without stopping, transgresses, and ex-

[7]Friedrich Nietzsche, *The Genealogy of Morals,* in *The Birth of Tragedy; The Genealogy of Morals,* trans. Francis Golffing (Garden City: Doubleday, 1956), Second Essay, chapter I, p. 189.
[8]*The Complete Works of Friedrich Nietzsche,* ed. Oscar Levy, (Edinburgh and London, 1910), vol. 5, part II, "The Use and Abuse of History," trans. Adrian Collins, p. 12.

ceeds, its limits.[9] "To die and to go beyond limits are moreover the same thing," writes Georges Bataille. "Of that being that dies in us, we do not accept the limits." And, "the ultimate meaning of eroticism is fusion, the suppression of the limit."[10]

In fact, the very concept of number, the only one in which Don Juan seems to believe, is defined only through the notion of *limit* that constitutes it. Even while defining, nevertheless, the order of the finite (de-finite), the limit also, by the same token, constitutes the order of the infinite. Thus, paradoxically, it is because number has a limit that it is, as such, infinite. Similarly, the series of women that Don Juan desires is *infinite* because it proceeds, in fact, from the *end* [*fin*], from the ceaseless passing of the *finite*, from the recurrent functioning of death in the figure of the new beginning itself, from the repetitive anaphoric rhythm: death/rebirth.

The Teaching of Rupture

That promise which my body made you I am powerless to fulfill.
        —Claudel, *The Satin Slipper*

Even as he transgresses limits and breaks promises, Don Juan is also teaching others, the victims of his seduction, to transgress limits themselves, to break their own promises first, before he breaks off his relations with them. It is important to note that, for all the women he seduces, accepting Don Juan's promise of marriage is possible only at

[9]Cf. *Don Juan, 1,* ii: "In this realm I have the ambition of the conquerors who fly ceaselessly from victory to victory, and who cannot resign themselves to *limiting* their desires. There is nothing that can *stop* the impetuosity of my desires: I feel I have a heart made for loving the whole world, and, like Alexander, I could wish that there were other worlds, so that I could *extend* my amorous conquests still further."

[10]Georges Bataille, *L'Erotisme* (Paris: UGE, Coll. 10/18, 1965), pp. 155, 156, 143.

the price of breaking a promise of their own. Elvira has to break her commitment to live in a convent, and Charlotte her promise to marry Pierrot. "You weren't born to live in a village," Don Juan says to Charlotte: "there is no doubt that you deserve better luck. Heaven . . . has led me here on purpose to prevent this marriage . . . whether I *tear you away* from this miserable place will depend entirely on you . . ."[11] (II, ii). In a single breath Don Juan proposes to *tear* Charlotte *away* from her origins, to *cut her off* from her class, to *make her break* with her fiancé. Thus Don Juan is not only a master but a professor of rupture. Even while making his own promises, he teaches the others, through the irony of their own behavior and through the needs of their flesh, that promises as such are liable to be broken.[12] Etymologically, "to seduce" signifies "to separate";[13] and Don Juan, true to that underlying meaning, seduces only by teaching that separation is an *essential* aspect of seduction. "The glance that took me in," Elvira tells him, "reveals much more to me than I want to know" (I, ii). Donjuanian perversity is thus above all a form of higher lucidity: cruelty, in Artaud's sense.

> Cruelty is above all lucid, a kind of rigid control and submission to necessity. There is no cruelty without consciousness and without the application of consciousness. . . . It is consciousness that gives to the exercise of every act of life its blood-red color, its cruel nuance, since it is understood that life is always someone's death.

[11]Cf. I, ii: "The person I am speaking of is a young fiancée . . . who was brought here by the man she has come to marry; by chance I saw this pair of lovers three or four days before their trip. I have never seen two people so happy with each other . . . ; my heart was struck, and my love began with jealousy. Yes, . . . I anticipated taking enormous pleasure in being able to *disturb their understanding, and break this attachment. . . .*"

[12]Thus, for example, in order to justify his about-face with respect to Elvira, Don Juan cynically brings forth a sort of ironic poetic justice by invoking the breaking of her own religious commitment: "I have had scruples, Madame, and I have opened my soul's eyes to what I was doing. It has occurred to me that, in order to marry you, I have stolen you away from the confines of a convent, that you have broken vows that were committing you in another direction . . ." (I, iii).

[13]From Latin *seducere,* to separate.

I have therefore said "cruelty" as I might have said "life" or "necessity."

Everything that acts is a cruelty.[14]

Molière's *Don Juan* is thus attached to the theater of cruelty to the extent that the play dramatizes the very cruelty of the performative: the cruelty of the speech act—the quintessential act of the speaking body—inasmuch as it comprises an ineluctable necessity of rupture or break.

The Donjuanian Cutting Edge

And so I am not the master of my life, I am only one thread among many which must be woven into the fabric of life! Very well, if I cannot spin, I can at least cut the thread.
　　　　　　　　　　　　—Kierkegaard,*Either/Or*

It is doubtless no accident that Don Juan, master of rupture and theoretician of the breach, lives at swordpoint, wielding a weapon that strikes and slices and excelling in its use.

DON CARLOS: . . . One can see, by the flight of those thieves, how much we owe to your arm. . . . [III, iii]

DON JUAN: You know . . . that I know how to use my sword when it is called for. [V, iii]

It is no accident, either, that the entire play culminates, in the next-to-last scene, just before Don Juan is finally swallowed up, in a sort of dueling match between Don Juan and a ghost, the "Ghost as a veiled woman":

[14]Antonin Artaud, *The Theater and Its Double,* trans. Mary Caroline Richards (New York: Grove, 1958), pp. 102, 173, 130.

DON JUAN: Ghost, phantom, or devil, I want to see what it is.
(*The Ghost changes form, and represents Time with his scythe in his hand.*)
SGANARELLE: O Heaven! Do you see this change in form, Sir?
DON JUAN: No, no, nothing is capable of impressing me with fear; and I want to test with my sword whether it is a body or a spirit.
(*The Ghost flies off while Don Juan is seeking to strike it.*)
[v,iv]

In a brilliant image, Molière emblematizes here the very essence of the Donjuanian act as struggle, or dramatic confrontation, between two cutting instruments: Time's scythe, and Don Juan's sword. In making cuts, the Donjuanian performance is seeking above all to cut off the advance of Death, to escape Time, to cut away from its cutting edge: it strives to *cut out Time's cutting*. If Don Juan *misses* the Ghost—of woman or of Time ("The Ghost flies off while Don Juan is seeking to strike it")—, if his sword or his performance only results here, literally, to return to Austin's vocabulary, in a *misfire,* a "missed stroke," it is because the possibility of *missing*—as it is represented by the cutting of Time's scythe—is at work within the domain of the performative. The Don Juan myth thus deals with the performative in such a way as to bring to light this breach inherent within it.

The Fastest Runner, or the Space of a Movement

The breach or break is, in reality, the structuring principle of the Don Juan myth. The lack of structure of Molière's play has often been criticized, along with the absence of connections between scenes. But such criticism fails to see that in this play breaks constitute, paradoxically, the connecting principle itself. Just as, in order to continue, Sganarelle asks Don Juan to be so kind as to interrupt him—"Oh, *dame*, interrupt me then. . . . I'd be unable to argue, if no one interrupted me" (III, ii)—in just this same way the whole play, in harmony with the spirit of the myth, is subtly organized as a continuity of breaches, as a structured system of the repetition of breaks.

However discontinuous it may be, the sequence of scenes delineates the direction of a trajectory, indicates the direction of Don Juan's movement. From the very beginning of the play, in fact, Don Juan is characterized as the one who, by definition, is always in motion, never stops. "I . . . know your heart to be the greatest runner in the world," Sganarelle says to him. "It enjoys strolling from one bond to another, and hates to remain in one place" (I, ii). Don Juan is the one who does not stay[15] [Fr. *demeurer*]—both in the spatial sense of remaining in one place, staying at home, inhabiting a place, and in the temporal sense of lasting, enduring, staying the course. Structuring the linking of scenes, Don Juan's discontinuous movement thus defines his double relation to space and to time.

Now from the very first scene on, it is precisely the meaning of this break with the dwelling-place that is in question and that poses a problem. "Would this unforeseen *departure* be an infidelity on the part of Don Juan?" asks Gusman (I, i). Baudelaire writes,

> But only those who leave for leaving's sake
> Are *travelers* . . .
> They never balk at what they call their fate.[16]

---

[15]Cf. I, ii: "DON JUAN: What? You think we should commit ourselves to *stay* with the first object that takes our fancy . . . ?" and II, ii (Don Juan to Charlotte): "You were not born to *stay* in a village." On the other hand, Sganarelle advises Charlotte to stay put (II, iv): "Don't be taken in by all the tales you hear; *stay* in your village."

[16]"Travelers," in *Les Fleurs du Mal*, trans. Richard Howard (Boston: Godine, 1982), p. 152.

Don Juan is a true traveler in the sense that he leaves for leaving's sake; he is the leavetaker who never deviates from his fate, the voyager who, advancing all the while, goes forward only to meet what is following and pursuing him. This paradoxical movement is staged by the structure of the play. The first act presents Don Juan as the pursuer pursued. This is the double meaning of the exposition: "A beauty has stolen my heart . . . I have *followed* her right to this town," Don Juan confides to Sganarelle, just as Sganarelle informs him that "Dona Elvira . . . , surprised by our departure, has set out to campaign against us" (I, ii). The pursuit of the new woman by Don Juan is thus presented, literally, as a *flight forward.* The relation of Don Juan to time, defined by the rhythmic, anaphoric antithesis, "death/renaissance," his flight in the face of "death" (which would imply fidelity to Elvira) and toward "falling in love," likewise determines his relation to space as the very tension of the opposition—but also as the vanishing point, even as the incessant displacement—between *behind* and *before,* in back and in front.

The second act repeats this double movement in reverse order. Throughout the act, Don Juan appears as the "maker of advances"—even when he is in the lead, he appears to be the follower and pursuer of women: the fiancée at sea, Mathurine, Charlotte. "This heart mustn't escape me," he says (II, ii). But at the end of the act, he is once more the one pursued. He is again obliged to leave in the face of a threat that comes from behind: La Ramée says, "Twelve men on horseback are looking for you . . . I don't know how they can *have followed you*" (II, v).

Nevertheless, in the third act, Don Juan's first encounters with Don Carlos and with the statue point up a shift in Don Juan's movements that puts them in a new light. Even as he runs away from death, which lies behind him in the person of his pursuers, Don Juan—noticing Don Carlos (whose identity he does not know) being attacked by thieves, runs forward to come to his aid. But Don Carlos is at that very moment himself in pursuit of Don Juan: "The author of this offense is a certain Don Juan Tenorio. . . . We have been looking for him for several days, and we *followed him* this morning," Don Carlos says to his rescuer (III, iii). Thus Don Juan unwittingly runs back toward his pursuers even as he moves ahead: what he is *escaping from* is exactly what he is *running toward*.

From this moment on, Don Juan is no longer master of the direction or meaning of his movement: heading toward the future, he moves toward the past. The same thing happens when Don Juan finds the Commander's statue along the fortuitous path of his forward flight, and seeks it out, taking the initiative of inviting it to dinner. In the final acts, what is behind—but encountered ahead—and what is past—encountered in the act of moving toward the future—turn back on Don Juan in the form of his pursuers (act III, Elvira's brothers; act IV, Monsieur Dimanche, Don Louis, Elvira; act v, Don Louis, the woman's ghost, the Commander's statue) and demand their due, insist that Don Juan pay his debts of fidelity, money, proper name, birth, life. Don Juan, a figure of flight and of displacement between death behind and death ahead, is finally cornered by the statue, the figure of immobility that calls a halt to Don Juan's own movement: "Stop, Don Juan" (v, vi.). Modeled on the paradoxes of the direction and meaning of Don Juan's movement, dramatizing these paradoxes, the eventful and discontinuous structure of Molière's play problematizes the relation of eroticism to time as a subversion of linear time and as a deconstruction of the *before/after* dichotomy and of the *behind/ahead* opposition.

The Haste Function:
The Temporality of the Promise

This temporal paradox likewise inhabits the promise, whose relation to time is particularly perverse. If Don Juan is indeed a "runner" ("I know your heart to be the greatest

runner in the world," Sganarelle says to him), his race—
ruled by urgency—is in reality a race against time:

> This love is quite hasty, no doubt; but what the hell! . . . one
> of them loves you as much in fifteen minutes as another one
> would in six months. [II, ii]

> A *pressing* matter forces me to leave here. . . . [II, v]

> Let's go. Bring me my supper *as soon as possible.* [IV, i]

> *Quick!* To supper. [IV, vii]

In the same way, promises are tied to a time of speed and
urgency, to what Lacan has called—in an entirely different
context—"the haste function," from which stems "the assertion of anticipated certainty." "It is a certain time," Lacan writes, "which is defined (in the two senses of taking its
meaning and finding its limit) by its end, at once goal and
termination."[17] Indeed, the Donjuanian promise, engendered by the anaphoric structure death/rebirth, is defined in
its turn by the end in these two meanings: by death, or life's
end, which life is fleeing, and by the satisfaction, the goal or
the end of desire, which life is pursuing. The promise, too, is
a flight forward, to the extent that it stems from the haste
function: between the limit and the end, vanishing point
between the end behind and the end ahead, it leaps across
the lack of/in the present toward an anticipation of the future, and across the lack of means toward an anticipation of
the end. Constituted by the act of anticipating the act of
concluding, the promise is symptomatic of the noncoinci-
dence of desire with the present. If Don Juan "fails to keep
his word,"[18] it is because his word, his promise, is at the
outset constituted by the act of failing, missing: missing
(failing) the present. Don Juan himself is thus only the
symptom of a perversity inherent in the promise.

[17]Jacques Lacan, *Ecrits* (Paris: Seuil, 1966), p. 205.
[18]"I don't understand," Gusman says, "how after showing so much . . .
impatience, . . . he could have the heart *not to keep his word*" [I, i].

The Act of Missing, or Repetition

In fact, the very act of missing appears, in the play, not only as the cause, as the condition of the promise's engendering, but also as the basis of its infinite repetition, since it is the Donjuanian mis-keeping of promises which gives rise to the series of threats and warnings, to the acts of commitment on the part of his pursuers who justify themselves by invoking Heaven's authority as a promise of justice. If promising consists in the production of an expectation (cf. Searle, *Speech Acts*, p. 232)—of meaning?—, the very disappointment of this expectation only perpetuates it, by bringing the acts of commitment back into play. Thus the entire drama is made of a signifying chain of promises which engender each other reciprocally, and whose connecting principle is their own failure to be kept.

Now it is precisely the repetition of promises that, in the Don Juan myth, subverts their authority. ("The performative utterance, being an act, has the property of being *unique*. It cannot be produced except in special circumstances, at one and only one time. / . . . Being an individual and historical act, a performative utterance cannot be repeated" (Benveniste, p. 236; his emphasis).

If Don Juan subverts the uniqueness of the promise by repeating precisely the promise of uniqueness—the promise of marriage, the supremely unique act—it is in order to ruin not the performance of language, but its *authority*. "A performative utterance . . . has existence only as an act of authority" (p. 236).

From what authority, then, does the performative emanate? Aside from explicit performatives, as Benveniste notes, "we must . . . admit as performatives utterances that are not obviously so because they are only implicitly attributed to the authority entitled to produce them" (p. 235). These are performative verbs reported "impersonally and in the third person": "*It is decided that . . .; The president of the republic decrees that . . . .* The utterance in the third person can always be reconverted into a first person and again assume its typical form" (p. 235). In the last analysis, the authority of the performative is nothing other than that of the first person. Now it is precisely the authority of the first person that Don Juan subverts, by parasitizing the performative through the infinite repetition of his promises of marriage. For the *first person,* too, takes its authority only from the ordinal hierarchy, from the founding value of the "first" in which, as we recall, Don Juan does not believe: once again, Don Juan thus deconstructs the First through Number. The multiplication of promises brings out the division inherent in the first person. The first person is thus itself subject to the cardinal law of number, that is, to the repetition of breaches.

The Promise of Consciousness

Don Juan sets himself in a parasitic relation to the promise—like that of symptom to thought, of the unconscious to consciousness: by bringing out, through repetition, the breach which is inherent in the promise but which it represses and conceals. On the contrary, every promise promises the completion of incompleteness; every promise is above all the *promise of consciousness,* insofar as it postulates a noninterruption, continuity between intention and act. To the extent that Don Juan embodies the performance of promising as a performance of rupture, he becomes the symptom of the self-subverting power of the performative. Indeed, the Don Juan myth is the myth of the performative only in that the performative, pushed to its extreme logical consequences, en*acts* its own subversion. What the myth of the speaking body, in other words, *performs,* is the very subversion of consciousness.

SGANARELLE: My reasoning is that there is something admirable in mankind. . . . Isn't it wonderful . . . that I have something in my head that thinks a hundred different things at this very moment, and makes my body do what it wants? . . .

(*He drops dizzily to the ground.*)

DON JUAN: There! Your reasoning has fallen flat on its face!

[III, i]

The Don Juan myth is in effect the myth of the promise of consciousness falling flat on its face.

Now the promise of consciousness is nothing but the promise of Heaven, the promise of the constative. Since Don Juan serves as the emblem, for his father at least, of a heavenly promise not kept, the question arises whether the end of the myth, Don Juan's death, which brings to fruition the warnings that invoked Heaven as a promise of justice, accomplishes the celestial commitment: will Heaven's promise concerning Don Juan be better kept by his death than it has been by his birth?

The Triple Dénouement, or
The Promise of Ending

Finished, it's finished, nearly finished, it must be
going to finish.

—Beckett, *Endgame*

It is no doubt significant that Don Juan's death does not constitute the end point of Molière's play, which has not one but three denouements: Don Juan's conversion to the social code of religion, his death at the statue's hands, and the appearance of Sganarelle demanding his lost wages. Like the promise of marriage, the end is generally that which by definition cannot repeat itself. Now if in Molière's play the end itself is multiple, it is because the Don Juan myth is precisely the myth of the repetition of the end. Just as there is no first number, there is no last number either. The last number itself is divided, doubled, multiplied.

Whereas the fantastic ending—the intervention of the statue—signifies Don Juan's loss, the realistic ending[19]—his false conversion—signifies on the contrary his "rescue" and his survival: "I want to take shelter (*me sauver*) in this favorable spot and protect my affairs," he announces (v, ii). On the one hand, then, the end as life is assured; on the other, the end as death. However opposed they may be, both endings dramatize the *disappearance of the Don Juan scandal*: dead rebel or live hypocrite, Don Juan will no longer scandalize the world.

If the very idea of ending that arises from this double conclusion is that of the resolution of scandal, the opposition of the two endings (life assured or death assured) seems to situate the scandal in Don Juan's incessant *vacillation* between the two, whereas the disappearance of scandal would consist, precisely, in *choosing* one or the other.

However, the first ending—the false conversion—does not really succeed in *ending*, in carrying out the idea of ending, or in resolving the scandal, since Don Juan's hypocrisy in reality only masks the scandal and makes it invisible as such: far from eliminating scandal, this hypocrisy reinforces and crowns it.

> SGANARELLE: Sir, what sort of devilish style are you taking on now? . . . I think that Heaven, which has put up with you up to now, won't be able to stomach this latest horror?
> DON JUAN: Don't worry, Heaven isn't as fussy as you think. . . . [v, iv]

Since the false conversion ending fails to accomplish the finality of the ending, a second conclusion is required: that of Don Juan's death, which, for its part, seems to eliminate

---

[19]See Jean Jaffré, "Théâtre et idéologie. Notes sur la dramaturgie de Molière," in *Littérature*, 3 (Feb. 1974), 71–72.

the scandal; in addition, its fantastic aspect dramatizes the symbolic elements of a kind of poetic justice: the Commander, representing both the authority of the Law that commands and that Don Juan flouts, and the return of the repressed, the haunting return of the supposedly dead past; the statue, the immobile figure of death that stops Don Juan's transgressive movement: "Don Juan, that's enough" (IV, viii); "Stop, Don Juan" (V, vi); the fire, representing the fire of desire through which Don Juan is consumed: "O Heaven! What do I feel? An invisible fire is burning me, I can't go on. My whole body is becoming a bed of live coals" (V, vi); Heaven, symbolically made concrete as a hole in the earth, a hole in reality: "Earth is opening and swallowing him up; and great fires are coming out of the place where he fell" (V, vi). "Thus Heaven is another stage," as Claude Reichler writes: "what is at stake, in *Don Juan*, is the irruption, within a spatial continuum, of a radical gap."[20]

The Dinner Invitation, or the Stone Feast

If I have any *taste*, it is for hardly anything but earth and stones.
                          —Rimbaud, "Feast of Hunger"

It is hardly an accident, either, that Don Juan's mythic death stems from a dinner invitation (Don Juan's to the statue, and the statue's to Don Juan). In the Don Juan myth, food stands for pleasure, insofar as it serves no purpose,[21] is

[20]Claude Reichler, "Don Juan jouant," in *Obliques*, 4, *Don Juan*, vol I., pp. 59, 60. See also Claude Reichler, *La Diabolie* (Paris: Minuit, Coll. "Critique," 1979).
[21]Cf. Jacques Lacan, *Encore* (Paris: Seuil, 1975), p. 10: "Pleasure is what has no purpose."

pure expenditure, aneconomic. Don Juan, who rejects the circular economic return of the debt,[22] is nevertheless the one who gives: who gives food, who gives pleasure.

Oh, say, Monsieur Dimanche, will you eat with me? [IV, iii]

Moreover, in the Don Juan myth, the very act of eating stems in its turn from the haste function. Now this function transmits anguish just as much as it does a desire for pleasure. It is in this way that, at the end of the last three acts, the more death closes in on Don Juan by way of his pursuers' threats, the more Don Juan is in a hurry to eat: for example, after the first encounter with the statue, in which the statue nods at him: "Let's go. Bring me my supper as soon as possible" (IV, i). Or when his father has just cursed him: "Will they bring my supper soon?" (IV, v). And after Dona Elvira's final warnings: "Quick! To supper." (IV, vii).

However, the Commander's statue, although it too has been invited to dinner and in turn invites Don Juan, does no more than "disturb his meal" (IV, vii). The term "stone feast"—the hermetic subtitle of Molière's play—can thus be understood as a reference to the stone of the statue itself: to the stone of the statue, insofar as it is a concrete image of Death, not only as *that which breaks the meal,* but as that which, by definition, *cannot be digested,* assimilated, or understood—that which the mouth cannot incorporate or appropriate.

From Mouth to Hand

It is not unimportant that Don Juan's fantastic death is thus associated with the mouth of an organ of pleasure. In a way, one might say that the Don Juan myth of the mouth is

[22]See Michel Serres, "Apparition d'Hermès: Don Juan," in *Hermès* 1: *La Communication* (Paris: Minuit, 1968).

the precise *place of mediation between language and the body*. Don Juan's mouth is not simply an organ of pleasure and appropriation, it is also the speech organ *par excellence*, even the organ of seduction. Thus it is only poetic justice if, in an indirect way, Don Juan dies, as it were, through the mouth—which ends up becoming the sign of the rupture in the speaking body itself. "What?", Don Juan said to Sganarelle after the announcement of his false conversion, "you take what I have just said at face value, and *you think my mouth was in agreement with my heart?*" (v, i).

The last symbolic gesture in Don Juan's fantastic execution is that of the fatal contact of his hand with the statue's:

> STATUE: Give me your hand.
> DON JUAN: Here it is. [v, vi]

This gesture accomplishes and crowns the poetic justice of the punishment, since "to give one's hand" also means "to marry," and since Don Juan's transgression consisted precisely in *giving his hand* over and over, in being "a marrier at every hand" (I, i).

The fantastic conclusion thus unfolds as a sort of dialectic between the don and his debt. If Don Juan dies, symbolically, for not having kept his promises, for not having respected his debts, for having refused to *give in return*, he dies no less through what he *gives:* Don Juan, who gives food, who gives his hand, who gives his word, dies while giving food, his hand, his word to the statue of death.

> STATUE: Stop, Don Juan: You gave me your word yesterday to come eat with me. [v, vi]

If the only word Don Juan keeps is the word he gives to the statue, is it because only death can seduce the seducer?

So Don Juan keeps the appointment: if he refuses to render up his debts, he ends up nonetheless rendering himself up, *rendering* his soul or his life. The debt is thus paid in the end. Heaven's promise appears to be kept. The scandal is eliminated.

Engagement and Wages

But why, at that point, do we have a third ending, a supplementary finality, from the mouth of Molière-Sganarelle himself,[23] in a last word suggesting that the second ending, Don Juan's death, in its turn has not succeeded in finishing, in bringing about the end?

> SGANARELLE: Ah! my wages! my wages! At last by his death everyone is satisfied: offended Heaven, broken laws, seduced girls, dishonored families, outraged parents, husbands at the end of their rope, everyone is happy. I'm the only one who is unhappy. My wages, my wages, my wages! [v, vi]

Don Juan has *paid*—with his life. But the debt remains unpaid nonetheless. The accounting is not over. We might think we hear Don Juan's mocking voice repeating from beyond the grave: "Don't worry, Heaven isn't as fussy as you think" [v, iv]. Precision exists only in arithmetic: "two and two are four, Sganarelle, and four and four are eight." But arithmetic has no meaning: the accounts cannot be added up, there is no final reckoning.

The third ending thus subverts the meaning of the second: if, according to the second ending (the fantastic outcome), Don Juan's death is just and, as such, carries out Heaven's promise to the letter (Heaven whose role is specifically to underwrite the contract and guarantee the payment of the debt), according to the third ending (Sganarelle's complaint), Don Juan's death is as unjust as his life. Death does not make *meaning*, since, on the contrary, it is death that prevents the payment of the debt, thus *breaking* the promise once again. Heaven's commitment is not kept. The wages are not paid.

Thus the three endings of Molière's play do not manage to keep the promise of ending itself: the promise of creating *meaning*, of bringing *satisfaction* to desire, of eliminating

[23]It is well known that Molière himself played the role of Sganarelle.

the scandal. Even through Don Juan's death, the scandal is not eliminated, since death is the greatest scandal of all. The scandal proves to be irreducible. And likewise the dissatisfaction, made concrete by Sganarelle's shouting about his lost wages. Far from rendering a meaning, the conclusion emblematizes the very space of meaninglessness. Far from bringing satisfaction, the conclusion dramatizes, again and always, both the lacking and the lack of means as anticipation of the end. Like Sganarelle, man remains alone on the stage, a player playing beyond his means, a valet deprived of his master. "Once one is *master*," as the seducer once said, "there is *no more to say* nor anything left to wish for" (I, ii). Mastery—or the satisfaction of desire—is thus a figure of silence. Now if the promise of ending does not succeed in realizing itself as *meaning*, it cannot realize itself as *silence*, either. Since man is a slave without a master, there will always be more to say, more to wish for, more to promise, more promises not to keep.

III

The Scandal of
the Performative

I am the promise that cannot be kept.
—Claudel

"When I make a word do a lot of work like that,"
said Humpty Dumpty, "I always pay it extra."

"Oh!" said Alice. She was too much puzzled to
make any other remark.

"Ah, you should see 'em come round me of a Sat-
urday night," Humpty Dumpty went on, wagging
his head gravely from side to side, "for to get their
wages, you know."

(Alice didn't venture to ask what he paid them
with; and so you see I can't tell *you*.)
—Lewis Carroll, *Through the Looking-Glass*

If the conceptual economy of the performative proves to govern the Don Juan myth in Molière's interpretation, might Molière's text in turn shed light on the theoretical, linguistic, and philosophical stakes in research on the performative? Might the question of the relation between the erotic and the linguistic—the Donjuanian problem *par excellence*—provide a way of looking at linguistics and analytic philosophy, might it in some way *inform* speech-act theory?

Austin's Donjuanism

It is striking to note that Austin's fundamental gesture, like Don Juan's, consists in substituting, with respect to utterances of the language, the criterion of *satisfaction* for the criterion of *truth.* "Truth and falsity are . . . not names for relations, qualities, . . . but for a dimension of assessment—how the words stand *in respect of satisfactoriness* to the facts . . . to which they refer" (*HT*, p. 149). Thus, like Don Juan, Austin too introduces into thinking about language the dimension of *pleasure*, quite distinct from that of knowledge; a dimension that is already implicit, moreover, in the success/failure criterion of linguistic performance—success or failure that Austin labels, significantly, "felicity" or "infelicity" of action.

Again like Don Juan, Austin, as philosopher and teacher, is above all an unbeliever and a demystifier, a theoretician of human error and illusion.

> I think that if we pay attention to these matters we can *clear up some mistakes in philosophy*; and after all philosophy is used as a scapegoat, it parades mistakes which are really the mistakes of everybody. [*PP*, p. 252]

> SGANARELLE: What, Sir, are you impious in medicine too?
> DON JUAN: It is one of the biggest mistakes men make. [III, i]

In fact Austin, like Don Juan, is not simply an unbeliever, he is an iconoclast, a destroyer of fetishes.

> What we need to do for the case of stating, and by the same token describing and reporting, is *to take them a bit off their pedestal*, to realize that they are speech acts no less than all these other speech acts that we have been mentioning and talking about as performative. [*PP*, pp. 249–250]

> I distinguish five very general classes: but I am far from equally happy about all of them. They are, however, quite enough to *play Old Harry with two fetishes which I admit to an inclination to play Old Harry with*, viz. (1) the true/false fetish, (2) the value/fact fetish. [*HT*, p. 151]

Like Don Juan, Austin takes into account a certain inconsistency, a certain capacity for *forgetting*—a forgetting that permits a new beginning:

> *Forgetting* for the time the initial distinction between performatives and constatives and the programme of finding a list of explicit performative words, . . . *we made a fresh start* by considering the senses in which to say something is

to do something. Thus we distinguished the locutionary act . . . ; the illocutionary act . . . ; the perlocutionary act. . . . [*HT*, p. 121]

Like Don Juan's life, Austinian research is thus modeled on anaphora, on repetition of beginnings.

If the beginning must itself begin again, it is because, in Austinian research as in the Don Juan myth, the promise of ending is not kept, satisfaction is not attained. Having posited the opposition between performative and constative and having, in a first stage, sought to define this opposition in terms of grammatical criteria alone, Austin concludes:

> Now this contrast surely, if we look back at it, is *unsatisfactory*. Of course statements are liable to be assessed in this matter of their . . . being true or false. But they are also liable to infelicity every bit as much as are performative utterances. [*PP*, pp. 247–248]

> Considerations of this sort, then, may well make us feel pretty *unhappy*. [*PP*, p. 247]

The fact that research itself comes to an *unhappy* ending (which by that very token it considers a nonending, a need to start all over again) may mean that research, subjected to the felicity/infelicity criterion, constitutes in itself a performance more than a statement, that it too belongs to the order of the performative rather than to that of the constative.

As performance, the Austinian enterprise is itself inhabited by a lack of means. Just as the Donjuanian act of promising is constituted, doubly, by the act of failing (both in the sense of failing in one's aim and in the sense of failing to keep one's word), the Austinian analysis, if it is an act, is only the act of *failing to grasp the constative of the performative*. How, indeed, might one find the truth of that which, as such, deconstructs the criterion of truth itself? Austin's distinction ends up subverting itself; Austin abandons the statement/performance opposition in favor of a generalized theory of the performative: the general doctrine of illocutionary acts. Like Don Juan, Austin takes into account the subversive, and self-subversive, potential of the performative.

The Question of the Ground

Now it is this self-subversion, this self-transgressive character of the Austinian performance that Benveniste cannot accept. Thus he distances himself from the general theory of illocution, in order to reestablish the sharp antithesis or opposition between constative and performative. "Whether or not [Austin] was right," Benveniste argues, "to set up a distinction and then immediately go about watering it down and weakening it to the point of making one doubt its existence, it nonetheless remains true that linguistic matter serves as a *basis* for the analysis in this case" (p. 234).

The stake in the debate that opposes Benveniste to Austin can thus be expressed in the following question: can the performative, as such, serve as the basis or *ground* for the theory? For Benveniste, the answer is yes, and the interest of the performative lies precisely in its capacity to serve as the basis for linguistic analysis. Austin, however, deconstructing—like Don Juan—the founding, originary value of the "first," is conscious in his turn of the fact that the very performance of the performative consists precisely in performing the loss of footing: it is the performance of the *loss of the ground*. Now the performance of the loss of grounds cannot itself serve as a ground; rather, as a basis, it can only subvert itself, cause the ground to give way beneath:

> I must explain that we are *floundering* here. To feel the *firm ground* of prejudice *slipping way* is exhilarating, but brings its revenges. [*HT*, p. 61[

Thus the Austinian relation to the performative instrument is not, as for Benveniste, a relation to a ground, but quite to the contrary a relation to a loss of ground, or of footing:

> We have discussed the performative utterance and its infelicities. That equips us, we may suppose, with two *shining new tools* to crack the crib of reality maybe. It also equips us—it always does—with two *shining new skids* under our metaphysical feet. [*PP*, p. 241]

In the eyes of its creator, the performative instrument, although tending toward the constative ("to crack the crib of reality"), is itself performative, that is, capable above all of the *act of failing*, of missing or of losing ground, an act itself constituted by the lack of means inherent in falling or skidding. My "reasoning has fallen flat on its face," Austin will declare in effect, as Don Juan does to Sganarelle.

Benveniste, however, refuses to agree that the Austinian code has fallen flat, refuses to write off this habit the performative has of failing in its own statement, of subverting its own consciousness. Like Sganarelle, he defends the authority of consciousness as he does the authority of the code:

> We see no reason for abandoning the distinction between the performative and the constative. We believe it justified and necessary, provided that one maintain it *within the strict conditions of use that sanction it*, without letting the consideration of the "result obtained" intervene since this is the source of confusion. [P. 238]

Significantly, Benveniste thus excludes from linguistics not only the general doctrine of illocutionary acts, that is, the generalized theory of the performative, the radical and total subversion of the constative as such, but also, and specifically, the theory of "infelicities," of failures. In regard to the Austinian analysis, and with a touch of astonishment, it would seem, Benveniste notes:

> The most important part of this article deals with the "un-happinesses" of the performative utterance, with the cir-cumstances which can render it null and void. . . . We have taken from this article only the most salient points of the line of reasoning and those arguments in the demonstration which touched upon facts which are properly linguistic. Thus we shall neither examine the considerations of the logical "unhappinesses" which can overtake and render in-operative either type of utterance, nor the conclusions Aus-tin was led to by them. . . . A performative utterance that is not an act does not exist. [Pp. 233–234, 236]

Benveniste's exclusion of the theory of failures is more than a technical convenience, more than a methodological *parti pris*. It is a fundamental gesture, philosophical in its import, which *situates* failure squarely *outside* of the per-formative, that is, both outside the language act and outside its theory. Now for Austin, the capacity for failure is situ-ated not outside but *inside* the performative, both as speech act and as theoretical instrument. Infelicity, or failure, is not for Austin an *accident* of the performative, it is inherent in it, essential to it. In other words, like Don Juan, Austin conceives of failure not as external but as internal to the promise, as what actually constitutes it.

Breach of Promise

That is why, like Don Juan, Austin suspects in his turn that the promise will not be kept, the debt not paid, the accounts not settled—that there will be no one to pay the wages. It is on this final suspicion, indeed, that he concludes his article "Performative Utterances":

> The notions that we have considered then, are the performa-tive, the infelicity, the explicit performative, and lastly . . . the notion of the forces of utterances. I dare say that all this

seems a little *unremunerative*. . . . Well, I suppose in some
ways it is *unremunerative*. . . . [*PP*, p. 251]

Subversive of the very opposition that it institutes and that
constitutes it, subversive then, in the last analysis, of the
constative authority of language, the performative *doesn't
pay*. Like the end of the Don Juan myth, the end of Austinian research does not manage to eliminate the scandal of
failures, of misfires, nor does it manage to dispel the lack of
satisfaction. But Benveniste, as a linguist whose project is a
constative, cognitive science of language, refuses to recognize such an unrewarding end. Indeed he voices a complaint,
like Sganarelle, over unpaid wages.

In effect, Benveniste reproaches Austin with nothing
short of his Donjuanism: his *inconstancy*, his infidelity to
his own beginning, to his own initial distinction. In other
words, Benveniste reproaches Austin for *failing to keep his
word:* for not keeping his promise of a constative of the
performative. *is it possible*

The Don Juan myth thus recounts for us the adventure of
modern linguistics in its confrontation with the philosophy
of language. Like Donjuanism, the philosophy of language,
in the face of linguistics, proves to be a subversive seduction. Austin is Benveniste's fool, as Don Juan is Sganarelle's.

Benveniste, as a linguist, establishes a limit in order to
respect it, that is, in order to *de-fine:* to classify, to distinguish, to construct. Austin, on the other hand, like Don
Juan, establishes a limit only to transgress[1] it, that is, to *in-*

[1]Cf., in Austin, the explicit *credo* of boundary-crossing, in his response—
and one could hardly ask for a more Donjuanian response—to Jean Wahl,
who had asked him the provocative question: "Is philosophy an island, or a
promontory? I mean simply that I often have the impression that one shuts
oneself up on a narrow strip of linguistic territory, debars oneself from
going outside it. . . ." "Is philosophy," echoes Austin, "an island or a promontory? If I were looking for an image of this kind, I think I should say that
it's more like the surface of the sun—a pretty fair mess. You disentangle
yourself as best you can with the means you have at hand. Psychology,
sociology, physiology, physics, grammar, can all be pressed into service.
Philosophy is always breaking out of its frontiers and into neighbouring

fine: to declassify, to disarticulate, to deconstruct. Thus at the end of its argument, the philosophy of language *invalidates* its own hypotheses, whereas at the end of *its* argument linguistics *validates* its own hypotheses. As a promise of science, linguistics is a promise respected and kept. As a promise of consciousness, philosophy is a promise that cannot be kept.⌋

Like linguistics, literature believes in meaning; like the philosophy of language, it deconstructs its own belief. Between the authority of the broken promise and the authority of the promise believed in, between Sganarelle and Don Juan, Benveniste and Austin, literature is precisely *the impossibility of choice:* the impossibility of keeping the promise of meaning, of consciousness; the impossibility of not continuing to make this promise and to believe in it. Even as literature, through the figure of Don Juan himself, deconstructs its own seductiveness, it goes on seducing; but it promises nothing except that it will continue to promise.

---

territories. . . . Where is the boundary? Is there one anywhere? You could ask the same question about the four quarters of the horizon. There is no boundary. The field is wide open to anyone who chooses to enter it; first come, first served, and good luck to anyone who is the first to hit on something worthwhile": J. L. Austin, "Performative-Constative," in *Philosophy and Ordinary Language,* ed. Charles E. Caton (Urbana: University of Illinois Press, 1963), pp. 41–43.

A note by translator G. J. Warnock (p. 22) explains that this article "is a straightforward translation of Austin's paper 'Performatif-Constatif,' which he wrote in French and presented at a (predominantly) Anglo-French conference held at Royaumont in March 1958. The case of the discussion which follows it is somewhat more complex. The actual discussion at Royaumont was carried on in both French and English. What appears in the published volume after Austin's text (*Cahiers de Royaumont, Philosophie* No. IV, *La Philosophie Analytique*: Les Editions de Minuit, 1962, pp. 271–304) is a version of this, based on a transcript but substantially cut and edited, in which the contributions originally made in English were translated into French by M. Béra. . . . It seemed to me preferable simply to translate into English the entire French text, mainly for the reason that it is this edited version, and this only, that all those taking part are known to have seen and approved for publication."

Further quotations from Warnock's English translation will be identified as such; direct translations from the extended discussion transcribed in the *Cahiers de Royaumont* will be identified henceforth by the abbreviation *CR.*

Literature, the aporetic space between Don Juan and Sganarelle, is an interminable dialogue between the voice of the dead master and the voice of the servant who lacks a master, answering each other across the abyss, still prolonging their feast of language: a feast of pleasure—and of stone.

IV

Knowledge and Pleasure, or the Philosopher's Performance (Psychoanalysis and the Performative)

So runs the signifier's answer, above and beyond all significations. "You think you act when I stir you at the mercy of the bonds through which I know your desires. . . . So be it: such will be your feast until the return of the stone guest I shall be for you since you call me forth."

—Lacan, "Seminar on 'The Purloined Letter'"

What I call linguistics requires psychoanalysis in order to be sustained. I shall add that there is no other linguistics but linguistery.

—Lacan, "Toward a New Signifier"

In the foregoing pages I have tried to *do* things with Austin's *words*: I have sought to bring to light—by putting it to work—the fecundity of the performative, grasping it in its passage through the literary "thing."

I had better declare at once that I am *seduced* by Austin. I like not only the openness that I find in his theory, but the theory's potential for scandal; I like not only what he says, but what he *"does* with words." And it is the import of this *doing* (as distinct from the saying, from the simple theoretical statement) that I want now to articulate. After having done things with what he says, I shall try to say what he does.

To say what he does *with* what he says: for it seems to me that the history of linguistic philosophy—the history of Austin's influence and of the theoretical consolidation of his thinking about the performative—reflects an appropriation of the constative aspect of the theory, but hardly at all of its performative aspect. Although Austin was constantly asking what we *do* with (or through) what we say, the history of ideas has never inquired into what *Austin* was doing with what he was saying.

I should thus like to open a theoretical reflection on this misunderstanding by the history of ideas (on how to read its misreadings), seeking at the same time to demonstrate—on the basis of the foregoing analysis—the rich originality, the unique position (as I see it) not so much of Austinian *theory* as of the Austinian *"thing"* (a "thing" that is done, indeed, "with words"[1]), and its possible contributions to current theory.

The Status of the Referent, or, What Is Reality?

If a word which I use is to have meaning, I must "commit myself" by its use. If you commit yourself, there are consequences.

—Wittgenstein

Through its opposition, in turn, to structural linguistics (which arose out of Saussurian theory) and to transformational grammar (which has sprung from Chomskyan theory)—both of which reject the question of the referent as foreign to linguistic reality (i.e., to the linguistic system)—the theory of the performative reintroduces the problem of the referent into linguistics. Austin insists repeatedly on the fact that his research is aimed not solely at language but also at referential reality:

> We use words as a way to understand better the *overall situation* in which we find ourselves led to make use of words. I hope in this way I have answered the question: "Do we go beyond words?" [*CR*, p. 334]

[1]For an explanation of my concept of "thing," see Shoshana Felman, *La Folie et la chose littéraire* (Paris: Seuil, 1978; translation forthcoming from Cornell University Press); see also S. Felman, "La chose littéraire," in *Ornicar?*, no. 16 (Fall 1978); and S. Felman, "La chose littéraire: Sa folie, son pouvoir," in *Tel Quel*, 80 (Summer 1979).

To what extent do we use criteria that are not strictly linguistic? To what extent do we study phenomena that are not simply language phenomena? ... What we do ... specifically is ask ourselves *in what circumstances* we would use each of the expressions we are looking at. ... Language serves as a go-between so that we can observe the facts of life, which constitute our experience, and which we would be all too inclined not to see, without it. [Pp. 332–333]

It is not enough, however, simply to state, as linguists and theoreticians of language often do, that "reference plays a major role in performative utterances,"[2] as if from that point on one knew what "reference" was, as if its reintroduction would suffice to keep the status of reality from remaining a problem in language. This is an example of the hypnotic effect of the Austinian notions of *context, situation,* or *circumstances* (of the speech act), notions that, once introduced, are repeated as if they were themselves directly referential and as if, on the basis of these notions, the relation of reality to language became transparent, self-explanatory.

Things are much more complex than that. It seems to me that what it is important to see—what Austin's heirs have perhaps lost sight of—is not so much the reintroduction of the referent in the performative, but rather the *change of status* of the referent as such.

This change of status—which Austin does not articulate explicitly or conceive of directly, but which can nevertheless be analyzed, thought through on basis of his text—this change seems to me signally apt to converge or coordinate with the change of status of the referent in an apparently quite different field, that of psychoanalysis.

Like performative analysis, psychoanalysis too looks into the relation between words and acts, between language and referent: the interference and the interaction between real-

---

[2]Paul Larreya, "Enoncés performatifs, cause et référence," in *Degrés*, I, no. 4, (Oct. 1973), p. m/I.

ity and the signifier constitute the specific locus of its work, and of its questioning. Now it seems to me that three common features define the theoretical novelty—or the conceptual transformation—of the status of the referent in the field of psychoanalysis on the one hand and in the area of the performative on the other.

1. Material Knowledge of Language

According to both theories, the referent cannot be attained directly; it can only be approached or aimed at through the intermediary of language, which alone carries with it—at the very heart of its material functioning—a kind of knowledge having to do with reality: "The only knowledge is knowledge of languages," Lacan has said.[3] And Austin:

> If a language has lasted . . . , if it has been capable of serving in all circumstances of life through the ages, it is probable that the distinctions it marks, like the connections it makes . . . are not . . . without value. Things will be found in language . . . that concern all aspects of life, looked at from every angle and with the most divergent aims . . . and that are, all things considered, infinitely richer . . . than the types of day-dreaming I used to indulge in between lunch and tea-time, when I was testing my capacity to resolve the riddles of the universe as our good masters used to encourage us to do. [*CR*, p. 334]

Contrary to the traditional conception of the referent, however, referential knowledge of language is not envisaged here as constative, cognitive knowledge: neither for psychoanalysis nor performative analysis is language a *statement* of the real, a simple reflection of the referent or its mimetic representation. Quite to the contrary, the referent is itself

---

[3] Jacques Lacan, "Vers un signifiant nouveau" (Le Séminaire de Jacques Lacan), in *Ornicar?*, nos. 17–18 (Spring 1979), p. 14.

produced by language as its own *effect.* Both the analytic act and the performative are language effects—but referential language effects. This means that between language and referent there is no longer a simple opposition (nor is there identity, on the other hand): language makes itself part of what it refers to (without, however, being all that it refers to). Referential knowledge of language is not knowledge *about* reality (about a separate and distinct entity), but knowledge that *has to do with reality,* that acts within reality, since it is itself—at least in part—what this reality is made of. The referent is no longer simply a preexisting *substance,* but an *act,* that is, a dynamic movement of modification of reality.

2. Dialogic Reference

Both in psychoanalysis and in the field of the performative, the referential aspect arises—and can arise only—in a dialogic situation: that of analytical practice on the one hand, that of illocution and perlocution on the other. The referent functions dynamically, in an intervening space; radically bound—in its analytic impact as well as in its performative impact—to a structure of effects, it can inscribe itself only as an effect of structure: as a relation to a relation. Whereas, traditionally, the referent is conceived—as an entity identical to itself—in relation to a univocal and monologic language, the analytic or performative referent is attained, in language, only through a radically dialogical treatment of language.

Indeed, if the referential refers to the material reality of dialogue, that of *enunciation* (of "analytic discourse," or else that of language "performance," of which the referent is, literally, the very act of utterance), this is the case insofar as an utterance is always, irreducibly, *in excess* over its statement. Lacan writes: "What am I aiming at, if not at convincing you that what the unconscious brings back for us to study is the law according to which utterance can never be

77

reduced to the statement of any discourse?" (*Ecrits*, p. 892). It is precisely this excess of utterance over the statement it makes that Austin christens "illocutionary force" or "force of utterance,"[4] attempting, as he stresses, to contrast *force* and *meaning*. With respect to the system of meaning, the referential excess of utterance would thus be a sort of energizing "residue." Austin's particular emphasis on "force of utterance" as the referential residue of meaning does not always survive in translation. The French translator of the English philosopher chose to render the notion of "force" [*force*] by that of "value" [*valeur*],[5] a translation that unfortunately obscures a key term of Austinian thought. More generally, the French tendency—in Benveniste's wake, no doubt—is to refer to the central concept of Austinian theory by the term *énoncé performatif* ("performative statement").[6] Now Austin was not talking about *statement*,[7] but about *performative utterance* [*énonciation performative*]. To suppress, on the one hand, his specific emphasis on *utterance* and, on the other hand, his emphasis on *force*, is in fact to run the risk of giving rise to the misunderstanding we have encountered in the history of ideas—the risk of muting not only the concept of force and the concept of utterance, but Austin's own utterance and the force of his own discourse: his own illocutionary force.

There is more: the theoretical misunderstanding includes this last aspect of the transformation, in Austin's work, of the status of the referent. When Benveniste refers to "per-

---

[4] "The performance of an act *in* saying something as opposed to performance of an act *of* saying something" (*HT*, p. 99).

[5] *Quand dire c'est faire*, trans. Gilles Lane (Paris: Seuil, 1970).

[6] See Benveniste, *Problems in General Linguistics*; Oswald Ducrot, "Les énoncés performatifs," in "De Saussure à la philosophie du langage," introduction to the French translation of John R. Searle's *Speech Acts: Les Actes de langage* (Paris: Hermann, 1972), p. 11; Larreya, "Enoncés performatifs."

[7] Austin never once uses the expression "performative statement": it would be a contradiction in terms, to the extent that his efforts are wholly oriented toward questioning the very notion of "statement," toward insistence on the nonsymmetry of the utterance/statement opposition, insofar as *utterance*, and in particular *performative utterance*, is not exhausted by *statement*.

formative utterances" as *énoncés performatifs*, the term *énoncé* is justified by the fact that the performative is, as he emphasizes, "self-referential," that the statement uttered is the *equivalent*, here, of the utterance that it *denominates*:

> An utterance is performative in that it *denominates* the act performed. [P. 237; Benveniste's emphasis]

> This leads us to recognize in the performative a peculiar quality, that of being *self-referential*, of referring to a reality that it itself constitutes. . . . As a result of this it is both a linguistic manifestation, since it must be spoken, and a real fact, insofar as it is the performing of an act. The act is thus identical with the utterance of the act. The signified is identical to the referent. . . . The utterance that takes itself as a referent is indeed self-referential. [P. 236; Benveniste's emphasis]

According to Benveniste, since the referentiality of the performative is perfectly specular or self-reflexive ("self-referential"), the performative produces perfect *symmetry* between meaning and reference, like that between statement and utterance. "The act is thus identical with the utterance of the act. The signified is identical to the referent." The (performative) utterance is the mirror image of the (performative) statement.

This reasoning is not without relevance, and yet it draws false implications from Austin's thought. The performative is indeed self-referential, but for Austin this does not mean that it refers to an exhaustive specularity or to a perfect symmetry between statement and enunciation. On the contrary, it is from *asymmetry* that Austin's thought proceeds, from the *excess* of utterance with respect to statement, from "force of utterance" as a—referential—residue of statement and meaning.

What we have to understand on the basis of Austin's thinking about the status of the referent is that, in the final analysis, the performative has the property of subverting the alternative, the opposition, between referentiality and self-referentiality. If the language of the performative refers to itself, produces itself as its own reference, this language effect is nonetheless an action, an action that exceeds language and modifies the real: self-referentiality is neither perfectly symmetrical nor exhaustively specular, but produces a *referential excess,* an excess on the basis of which the real leaves its trace on meaning. |

The myth of Don Juan says just the same thing. If Don Juan abuses the performative by exploiting the self-referential capacity of language in order to produce referential illusions by means of self-referentiality, the very act of producing referential illusions itself overflows and reaches toward referentiality. And no doubt the outcome of the myth, the very figure of the statue that *takes Don Juan at his word,* is a symbolic way of expressing the hold—the empire—of the referential over and within Donjuanian speech, the impress or the trace that the real leaves upon meaning.

Moreover, Don Juan himself suspects the referential excess of his speech: if his *seductions* proceed from self-referential language acts and from specular meaning effects, it is from the referential excess of the specular that he draws his *pleasure* and his power over the others: from precisely that excess of the "force" of his speech over its meaning.[8] Paradoxically, Don Juan turns himself into a theoretician of language acts only because he is uninterested in language, because he is interested only in the heteronomy of the real. A lucid seducer, he takes perverse pleasure in producing at one

[8]Thus in the scene with the poor man who asks for alms, promising to "*pray* to Heaven all day long for the prosperity" of the giver, Don Juan maliciously seeks to pervert the sense of the speech act addressed to God, by replacing the performative of *prayer* with that of *blasphemy:* "I'll give you a gold piece in a moment, if you are willing to *swear* . . . Come on, you have to *swear*" (iii, iii). Now Don Juan seems to be saying something like this: "Blasphemy is as good as prayer, it is just as devoid of referential value, *it is only a speech act,* and one speech act is as good as another," but in reality he is not interested in the *meaning* of the act (whether blasphemy or prayer) and *is interested only in its referential value:* that of attesting to his power over the poor man (that is, the referential effect of his own seductiveness, the perlocutory power of his own language).

80

and the same time a meaning effect and a radically hetero-nomous reference effect, and in *confusing* the one with the other. The *Don Juan effect* is, pragmatically, that of confusion between meaning and reference, and, theoretically, that of problematization, of subversion of the dichotomy between self-referentiality and linguistic referentiality.

Like Don Juan, Austin is interested—through the optic of the performative—only in the referential excess of the self-referential operation, even as he deconstructs the opposition between the two.

And Benveniste reproaches him, here again, for his Donjuanism, by proposing to exclude from the theory of the performative the criterion—a justly Donjuanian criterion—of the "result obtained," which is the "source of confusion":

> And so we see no reason for abandoning the distinction between the performative and the constative. We believe it justified and necessary, provided that one maintain it within the strict conditions of use that sanction it, without letting the consideration of the "result obtained" intervene since this is the source of confusion. If one does not hold to precise criteria of a formal and linguistic order, and particularly if one is not careful to distinguish between sense and reference, one endangers the very object of analytic philosophy; the specificity of language. . . . [P. 238]

Here again, psychoanalysis is on Austin's side, and Don Juan's. The dialogic status of the analytic referent and the fact that "utterance will never be reduced to the statement of any discourse" destroy the opposition between the self-referential property of language and its referential property, which is not constative but performative. The real is not the negative reflection—the symmetrical opposite—of the specular: the two are *knotted together*. But the specular does not exhaust the real. The self-reflectiveness of consciousness, the linguistic self-referentiality of subjectivity no longer refer to an identity, but to a referential residue, to a performative excess.

3. The Dimension of Misfire

The third feature common to analytic theory and Austinian theory, with respect to the transformation of the status of the referent, consists in the fact that referentiality—analytic or performative—can be reached and defined only through the dimension of failure: on the basis of the *act of failing.*

We have seen the importance and the impact of the act of failing ("failing to keep one's word," "failing in one's attempt") in the Don Juan myth. We have seen, furthermore, the fundamental importance in Austin's thinking of *misfires,* along with the other failures or infelicities that may befall the speech act. Austin's famous insistence on the notions of "situation" and "circumstances," of "context" (of speech performance) that the analysis must take into consideration—notions in which the truly referential aspect of performative theory are ordinarily located—he introduced only on the basis of his examination of "misfires" and "infelicities" (see *HT,* Lecture ii). If the capacity for misfire is an inherent capacity of the performative, it is because the act as such is defined, for Austin, as the capacity to *miss its goal* and to *fail to be achieved,* to remain *unconsummated,* to *fall short* of its own accomplishment.

Austin does not speak, at least not explicitly, of "misfires" in the specifically analytical sense of parapraxis [in French, *acte manqué*]. But one can see how his grasp of the referential aspect of the act in negative terms is close, despite many differences, both to the Freudian concept of slip and parapraxis, and to the Lacanian concept of the differential referential, or the negative power of the real: "the real is the impossible."

For in psychoanalysis, as in the domain of the performative, the real is defined exclusively in terms of "misfires." Lacan writes:

> It fails. That's objective. . . . It's even so striking that it's objective that it is on this point that we have to anchor, in analytic discourse, the status of the object. Misfiring is the

object. . . . *The object is a misfire. The essence of the object is misfiring.* [*Encore,* p. 55]

What characterizes, at the level of the signifier/signified distinction, the relation of the signified to what is present as an indispensable third party, namely the referent, is properly enough *that the signified misses it. The collimator doesn't work.* [*Encore,* p. 23]

On this latter aspect of the transformation of the theoretical status of the referent, the encounter between psychoanalysis and performative analysis might be particularly fruitful for clearing up a misunderstanding that frequently arises in the usual interpretation of Lacanian theory. The notion of "lack" is often hypostasized as being central to Lacan's thought; it is believed that, for Lacan, the referent is the "lack,"[9] which to some observers links Lacanian theory, by a simple specular reversal, to the traditional conception of the referent as substance, to the "metaphysics" of presence.

But in reality this common interpretation itself misses the dimension of the "lack," or rather of "failure" [*manquement*] in Lacan. The comparison with Austin is particularly enlightening: for no more than Austin does Lacan deal with the *lack*, but rather with the *act of lacking* or *missing* (failing, misfiring, falling short: "the collimator doesn't work"), which is entirely different from the "lack." "We shall see how by means of repetition, as repetition of deception, Freud coordinates experience, *qua* deceiving, with a real that will henceforth be situated in the field of science, situated as that which the subject is condemned to miss, but even this miss is revelatory."[10]

[9]The lack of phallus, or the phallus as signifier of the lack.
[10]Jacques Lacan, *The Four Fundamental Concepts of Psycho-analysis,* ed. Jacques-Alain Miller, trans. Alan Sheridan (New York: Norton, 1978), p. 39. This translation of *Les Quatre Concepts fondamentaux de la psychanalyse, Le Séminaire XI* (Paris: Seuil, 1973) will be designated in subsequent references by the abbreviation *FFC.* It is noteworthy that Lacan speaks here of *lacking* with respect to the repetition compulsion. Similarly, we have seen that, with Don Juan, it is precisely from the act of lacking (or missing, or failing) that the repetition of promises proceeds. See above, "The Act of Missing, or Repetition."

The difference between lack and failure might best be elucidated from Austin's perspective. Austin insists (specifically with respect to the *misfire,* the act of failing to achieve the act) that the act of failing is not a simple negation, a simple absence of presence (of substance), nor even a simple absence of act:

> If we offend against . . . the . . . rules . . . —that is if we, say, utter the formula [of the marriage ceremony] incorrectly, or if, say, we are not in a position to do the act because we are, say, married already . . . , then the act in question, e.g. marrying, is not successfully performed at all, does not come off, is not achieved. . . . We shall call in general those infelicities . . . by the name MISFIRES. . . . When the utterance is a misfire . . . , our act (marrying, &c.) is void or without effect, &c. . . .

> Two final words about being void or without effect. *This does not mean,* of course, to say *that we won't have done anything: lots of things will have been done*—we shall most interestingly have committed the act of bigamy—but we shall *not* have done the purported act, viz. marrying. [*HT,* pp. 15–17]

The act of failing thus opens up the space of referentiality—or of impossible reality—not because *something is missing,* but because *something else is done,* or because something else is said: the term "misfire" does not refer to an absence, but to the enactment of a difference.

Another common error concerning Lacanian theory consists in the belief (as opposed to the reproach of "phallocentrism" or of the "lack"-referent) that for Lacan, on the contrary, there is no referent (this idea is not only professed by certain Lacanian disciples, but is also often formulated as a reproach by American psychoanalysts): if the "unconscious," according to Lacan, "is structured like a language," and if, on the other hand, language can only "miss" the referent, is this not an invitation to understand that, for Lacan, "everything is language"?

Here, too, Austin's terminology can be grafted usefully onto Lacan's in order to undo such simplifications. No more than Austin does Lacan argue that "everything is language," but rather, quite to the contrary, he argues that language raises the question of its own limit, that language (like "woman") is *not-everything.* But this *"not-everything" is itself an act of language,* indeed it is precisely the act of failing: if the referent is traced in only on the basis of the signified's act of failing (the signified "misses" the referent: "the collimator doesn't work"), it is precisely insofar as *the self-referentiality of language fails to be realized* in a symmetrically exhaustive way; insofar as the statement does not exhaust (indeed as it *fails* to exhaust) the "force of utterance."

Theoretical Coincidences, or the Missed Encounter between Languages

One language among others is nothing but the sum total of the ambiguities that its history has allowed to remain. It is the vein that the real has deposited there throughout the ages.

—Lacan, "L'Etourdit"

"Do you know Languages? What's the French for fiddle-de-dee?"

"Fiddle-de-dee's not English," Alice replied gravely.

"Who ever said it was?" said the Red Queen.

—Lewis Carroll, *Through the Looking-Glass*

Between psychoanalysis (particularly in its Lacanian version) and performative theory (particularly in its Austinian version), there exist, then, on the cardinal points, what might be defined as theoretical *coincidences,* in the double sense of the word "coincidence": spatial-geometrical (two superimposed figures) and temporal-historical (two simultaneous elements—events that happen together through a convergence of circumstances due apparently to chance). In fact, between the two theories (which are more or less simultaneous) there is no historical or circumstantial relationship: the two theoreticians never met in actual fact, nor was either subject to the other's influence. The convergent features of their theories are thus, literally, coincidences.

Psychoanalysis teaches us, however, that coincidences, in the history of the subject, are governed not by chance but by another kind of logic, specifically that of the unconscious. Would the same thing not hold true for the overall history of ideas? Might not the history of thought itself be governed in its turn by a logic of the analytic type, of which "coincidences" would be both symptoms and signs?

To say that there are theoretical coincidences between Lacan and Austin is to say that something happens, in the history of thought, between languages, *between tongues.*

Between tongues: between bodies. For if languages are tongues, tongues are bodies—and as bodies they are deaf, and foreign to each other. One can be translated into another, but they are intrinsically *incapable of hearing, of understanding, one another.* "It is a fact," Lacan says, "that languages [les langues]—I write this *l'élangue*—can extend themselves to be translated one into another, but that the only knowledge remains knowledge of languages. The relationship is not translated in fact" ("Vers un signifiant nouveau," pp. 13–14). "If I have used the expression: the unconscious is structured like *a* language, it is because I wish to maintain that a language is not language. There is something in *language* that is already too general, too logical."[11]

Austin and Lacan are both products of their respective languages. Each works with, and takes into account, the

[11]"Le Symptôme," *Scilicet,* no. 6/7 (1976), p. 47.

concrete functioning of his own language. That is to say that they are both effects of the knowledge of their own languages.

Now performative knowledge of a language is untranslatable. As evidence of this we may take the difficulties—and the misunderstandings—of Lacan's discourse in Anglo-Saxon countries, like the difficulties—and the misunderstandings—that Austin's text has encountered in French-speaking countries. The French-English encounter at Royaumont on the subject of Anglo-Saxon "analytic philosophy," an encounter that was centered on the theoretical research of Austin and his colleagues, constitutes, in this sense, a spectacular and symptomatic example of the *impenetrability* of linguistic mentalities, of the radical heteronomy of the ways of thinking determined by languages foreign to each other.[12] It suffices to listen to the very style of the objections offered to the English philosophers, and to the (very different) style of the responses, in order to find proof of this linguistic heteronomy, to see how discussion becomes not only a dialogue of the deaf, but an explicit thematization of the *mis-understanding* between languages. For example, the French objections:

> JEAN WAHL: Is philosophy an island, or a promontory? I mean simply that *I often have the impression that one shuts oneself up on a narrow strip of linguistic territory,* and that one debars oneself from going outside it. . . . I believe that even in Oxford people study categories. . . . [Warnock trans., p. 41]

[12]See the introduction to the proceedings of the Royaumont colloquium, which notes this heteronomy: "This volume . . . reproduces, as faithfully as possible, most of the presentations and the substance of the discussions that took place during the colloquium that was held at Royaumont on the theme of 'Analytic Philosophy.' The subject . . . of this colloquium marks an *attempt at dialogue between two philosophies that,* for years, *have seemed unaware of each other:* that of the English Oxford school, known as 'analytic,' with a different strain represented by the United States, and that of the 'continentals' . . . *The reader may wonder whether the colloquium succeeded in bringing about a real dialogue.* If we limit ourselves to the immediate outcome, *doubts are in order. The oppositions were clearcut. The distances to be traveled were immense"* (*CR*, p. 7).

M. PERELMAN: I have the impression that there are reasonable beings outside of England and beyond those people who speak English, who likewise have very different expressions in their own language . . . we wish to go beyond a conception that would be uniquely the one that has been found to be important in English. . . . [*CR*, p. 345]

R. P. VAN BRENDA: I should like . . . to express my satisfaction at having heard . . . this emphasis on the negative attitude of analytic philosophy toward all the enterprises of continental philosophy. English philosophers obviously have an absolute right to be uninterested in what is happening elsewhere. . . . When we see each other, we are sometimes too polite, and not very honest. It is the simple truth, I think, to say that there are many continentals who have no real interest in your philosophy. And I dare say you have the same attitude toward the continentals. [*CR*, p. 344]

M. GEWIRTH: I am neither continental nor English. I have come here as a neutral observer . . . , geographically neutral. . . . On the one hand . . . , it seems to me that the English . . . have given us some solid reasons for believing that they are innocent of many of the things for which they have been reproached, and, in particular, of an abusive *linguicentrism*. . . . One cannot deny that the English affect a certain scorn toward what is happening in philosophy in the rest of the world. And this scorn astonishes us, even to the extent that certain of us wonder what criteria are required to reject in their entirety all other ways of conceiving of philosophy. It goes without saying, I think, that the English feel only mistrust with regard to the undertakings of a Heidegger. . . . I think that to understand what is happening . . . we have to stick with Mr. Austin's own declarations. Working in the concrete, with the building blocks, as it were, the English philosophers have not yet reached the point where they could say—and perhaps . . . they are little inclined by nature ever to arrive quite at this point—why, for what reasons summed up in a simple and general formula, they think what they think, and condemn or simply avoid any other conception of philosophy. [*CR*, pp. 369–370]

If the French objections articulate the discordance between linguistic mentalities, the lack of understanding or
the misunderstanding between languages, Austin's responses—through their typically English humor—both engage and *avoid* an encounter or confrontation with the
French questioning, and thus articulate in turn, in their
Donjuanian fashion, the gap or the nonconfrontation—indeed, the *missed encounter*—between English and French:

> Why should we be surprised at the distance that separates
> us? It is a fact that we have, on both sides, our feet on
> different ground. . . .
>
> I do not think it would be fair to say that we pass most of our
> time . . . stigmatizing anyone at all. But I suppose that we
> might be accused of the sin of not greeting people in the
> street. I grant you that it is a more serious lack of politeness
> in a certain sense than a direct provocation. One may plead
> attenuating circumstances: we are too busy. . . .
>
> Let me add that as far as quarrels go, we already have our
> hands full. . . . If we are a movement, or if we are thought to
> be a distinct trend in today's philosophy, it is surely because
> we have come to believe, no doubt wrongly, that our most
> immediate colleagues are the only ones with whom it is
> worth our while to disagree openly. . . .
>
> So if we are reproached for our unexpected impertinence,
> and for our manner of stigmatizing people without appear-
> ing to do so, "A thousand pardons, but time is flying,[13] and
> life is so short!" [*CR*, pp. 372–373]

Thus the French-English encounter at Royaumont makes
nothing quite so explicit as the missed encounter between
languages. This irreducible gap or *nonconfrontation* between different linguistic mentalities, this way languages

Constantius and performative ?

[13]A Donjuanian statement *par excellence.* Cf. above, "The Haste Function: The Temporality of the Promise."

have of "not greeting each other in the street" even though they may nod, of confronting without meeting, is also expressed, and just as explicitly, in another context of confrontation between French and Anglo-Saxon thought, a confrontation in which, once again, Austinian theory is at stake. It is by means of a reflection on this nonconfrontation that John R. Searle, Austin's most famous American "disciple," in fact introduces his "reply" to the Derridean critique of performative theory:[14]

> It would be a mistake, I think, to regard Derrida's discussion of Austin as a confrontation between two prominent philosophical traditions. This is not so much because Derrida has failed to discuss the central theses in Austin's theory of language, but rather because he has *mis*understood and *mis*stated Austin's position at several crucial points, as I shall attempt to show, and thus *the confrontation never quite takes place.*

> . . . I should say at the outset that I did not find his arguments very clear and *it is possible that I may have misinterpreted*[15] *him as profoundly as I believe he has misinterpreted Austin.*[16]

The fact that in what follows Searle indeed *misses* a number of Derridean arguments[17] only further confirms the basic nonconfrontation, the intrinsically missed encounter or the inherent misunderstanding between languages.

If, therefore, the confrontation between English and French has not really taken place, the inherent nonrelation-

[14]Cf. Jacques Derrida, "Signature Event Context" in *Glyph*, no. 1 (1977), pp. 172–197.

[15]Mis-understood, mis-stated, mis-interpreted: the same root as mis-fire. We have arrived once again at the question (the problematics) of the performance of the act of failing—of missing.

[16]John R. Searle, "Reiterating the Differences: A Reply to Derrida," in *Glyph*, no. 1 (1977), p. 198.

[17]Cf. Derrida's incisive and sophisticated response, "Limited Inc.," in *Glyph*, no. 2, (1977), in English, and in *Glyph* 2 (*Supplement*), the French version.

ship between languages, the *nonconfrontation*—at least on the subject of the performative—*has really taken place,* as an event, in the history of ideas.

If there are theoretical coincidences, then, between Austin and Lacan, these coincidences not only occur in the absence of historical influence, but, what is more, they exist on the far side of a gap or linguistic aporia: the theoretical *relation* takes shape here in spite of and across the inherent *nonrelation* of English and French. In fact, if Lacan and Austin—with the same taste for paradox and the same self-subverting consciousness of a breach, at every point, in knowledge—are concerned with the same thing, they explore this object only within the respective—and divergent—geniuses of their own language: the (ironically empirical and pragmatic) genius of English, or the (sophisticated, allusive, speculative) genius of French. This means that they say (more or less, on certain points) the same thing, but they say it in the specific ways in which English and French are nevertheless destined to *miss each other,* not to meet.

Now the theoretical relation seems to me all the more interesting in that it proceeds from this historical nonrelation; the theoretical *encounter* is in fact all the more rich in teaching and questioning in that it proceeds precisely from the nonmeeting, from the (theoretically and historically) missed meeting between languages. For might this meeting without meeting not be capable of pointing, precisely, toward what Lacan calls "the function of the *tuchè* [as if by chance], of the *real as encounter,* the encounter in so far as it may be missed, in so far as it is essentially the missed encounter . . ." (*FFC,* p. 55)? "For what we have in the discovery of psycho-analysis is an encounter, an essential encounter—an appointment to which we are always called with a real that eludes us" (*FFC,* p. 53). Now if "the real is that which always comes back to the same place—to the place where the subject in so far as he thinks, where the *res cogitans,* does not meet it" (*FFC,* p. 49), and if, on the other hand, the referent is what the signified misses or lacks, might not the real be likewise situated in the way languages *miss each other*, the way in which languages that are foreign to each other meet even as they fail to meet? The theoretical coincidences between Lacan and Austin might thus—to borrow Lacanian terms once again—point toward "those radical points in the real that I call encounters. . . . Reality is in abeyance there, awaiting attention" (*FFC*, pp. 55–56).

If languages fail to meet, it is because they are *self-referential*, because they act—they affect the real—only by referring each to itself. What remains *untranslatable*, what is missed from one language to another and what the passage between languages is always condemned to miss, is thus precisely the *performative* functioning of a language, the way a language has of referring to itself and at the very same time of missing its own self-referentiality, by carrying its referring beyond itself toward reality. Now if Lacan and Austin communicate at the very level of untranslatability, of the missed encounter between languages, it is because their theoretical thought is itself, above all, a linguistic *act*. And, although the linguistic body of their respective acts remains in fact untranslatable, the theoretical coincidences between them take place nonetheless at the very point where acts are articulated with language: where a theory of acts is thought within and through a language that constitutes an act.

Between Body and Language, or, What Is an Act?

Both psychoanalysis and performative theory have in fact as their object the *rethinking* of the human act. "Man is a political animal," as Aristotle said, already defining man by the very specificity of his *acts*. But it was Nietzsche, characterizing man not as a "political animal" but as a *promising animal* (which is, of course, not without relation to the "political animal"), who defined what is human more specifically not by acts but by *speech acts*; and not simply by speech acts but by the essentially paradoxical and problematic nature of the speech act: "Is [that] not man's true problem?"[18] We may say that psychoanalysis and performative analysis, as modern theories, both rethink, each in its own particular fashion, what the passage from Aristotle to Nietzsche implies.

"Several times," Mallarmé writes, "a Comrade came, the same, that other, to confide to me the *need to act*: . . . what did he mean exactly?"

> To unclench one's fists, in a breach of the sedentary dream, for a prancing face-to-face with the idea, as a desire strikes or moves: but the generation seems little agitated . . . by the concern for extravagating any body. . . .
>
> *To act* . . . signified, visitor, I understand you, philosophically, *to produce on many a movement that gives you in return the feeling that you were its cause, thus that you exist*: of which no one believes himself, at the outset, sure. . . . to determine a force in some direction, any whatsoever contradicted by several. . . .
>
> *Your act always applies itself to paper*; for to meditate, without traces, becomes evanescent, nor let instinct exalt itself in some vehement and lost gesture that you sought.[19]

Through its opposition to pure movement, the act, Mallarmé suggests here, is what *leaves traces*. Now there are no traces without language: the act is legible as such (that is, as effect, as reality effect) only within a context in which it is *inscribed*. The act is thus a sort of writing on the real: "Your act always applies itself to paper." There is no act without linguistic inscription.

[18]*The Genealogy of Morals*, trans. Francis Golffing (Garden City: Doubleday, 1956), p. 189.
[19]Mallarmé, "L'Action restreinte," in *Oeuvres complètes* (Paris: Gallimard, Coll. Bibliothèque de la Pléiade, 1945), p. 369.

That is what both psychoanalysis and performative theory have discovered; each in its own way explores acts as language effects. Whereas Austin studies speech acts directly, psychoanalysis (in transference, for example) studies speech itself as an acting out or *passage into action*; and, of course, studies such "passages into action" as speech effects or signifier effects.

If the problem of the human act thus consists in the relation between language and body, it is because the act is conceived—by performative analysis as well as by psychoanalysis—as that which problematizes at one and the same time the separation and the opposition between the two. The act, an enigmatic and problematic production of the *speaking body*, destroys from its inception the metaphysical dichotomy between the domain of the "mental" and the domain of the "physical," breaks down the opposition between body and spirit, between matter and language. "A body," Lacan says, "is speech arising as such" ("Le Symptôme," p. 50). And Austin:

> There is indeed a vague and comforting idea in the background that, after all, in the last analysis, doing an action must come down to the making of physical movements with parts of the body; but this is about as true as that saying something must, in the last analysis, come down to making movements of the tongue. . . .
>
> We need to realize that even the 'simplest' named actions are not so simple—certainly are not the mere makings of physical movements, and to ask what more, then, comes in . . . and what does not . . . , and what is the detail of the complicated internal machinery we use in 'acting'. [*PP*, pp. 178–179]

The indissoluble relation between the physical and the linguistic, between body and language, act and discourse, turns out to be at the center of the cardinal myth that psychoanalysis has taken as its theoretical springboard: the tragedy of *Oedipus Rex*. When Oedipus utters his curse against Laius's murderer, and when the chorus holds that no one will escape this curse, for no one—including the criminal—will be capable of not being *afraid* of it, Oedipus speculates that "the man who in the *doing* did not shrink will fear no *word.*"[20] That assumption seems to me to be crucial if we are to understand what is being *played out*—what is at stake—in the tragedy of Oedipus. For it so happens that "fear" is attached here not to the "doing," to the act, but to the linguistic consequences of the act—to the *juncture* of "act" and "words." The source of the tragic consists not in the act, but in the encounter (at first missed, then gradually accomplished) between act and language. Laius's murderer, in fact, "in the *doing* did not shrink," but does come to fear the *speech act*: the curse of Oedipus.

The tragic, according to Aristotle, always stems from an act; it is in the act as such that the essence of tragedy lies:

> Tragedy is essentially an imitation, not of persons, but of action and life, of happiness and misery. All human happiness or misery takes the form of action; the end for which we live is a certain kind of activity, not a quality. Character gives us qualities, but it is in our actions—what we do—that we are happy or the reverse. . . . A tragedy is impossible without action.[21]

Might we once again modify Aristotle's definition with a Nietzschean annotation, noting that the essence of tragedy might be not the act, but rather the speech act, that in any case the tragic act *par excellence* turns out to be not murder but a speech performance? In *Oedipus Rex*, the tragedy *takes effect* only from the speech act: from the *curse* by means of which—unwittingly, and through his own words—Oedipus *acts* against himself. Similarly, in *Hamlet*, the tragedy stems from the *act of swearing* to which the

[20]Sophocles, *Oedipus the King,* trans. David Grene, in *The Complete Greek Tragedies,* vol. II: *Sophocles* (Chicago: University of Chicago Press, 1959), p. 22.
[21]Aristotle, *De Poetica,* in *The Works of Aristotle,* ed. W. D. Ross (Oxford: Clarendon Press, vol. XI, 1924), ch. VI, 1450a.

ghost commits Hamlet, from the *oath* taken by Hamlet—as by Oedipus—to "remember": not to forget the crime or the murder, and to avenge the slain father.

If the language act turns out thus to be at the root of *tragedy*, it proves to be in just the same way—as Molière's *Don Juan* attests—at the root of *comedy*. The tragic and the comic both stem in fact from the relation between language and body: a relation consisting at once of incongruity and of inseparability. The speaking body is *scandalous* precisely to the extent that its *performance* is, necessarily, either *tragic* or *comic*.

Now if the theory of the performance of the speaking body—of speech acts proper—lies in the realm of the performative, the theory of the scandal of this performance falls in the domain of psychoanalysis. The scandal consists in the fact that the act cannot *know what it is doing*,[22] that the act (of language) subverts both consciousness and knowledge (of language). The "unconscious" is the discovery, not only of the radical divorce or breach between act and knowledge, between constative and performative, but also (and in this lies the scandal of Austin's ultimate discovery) of their undecidability and their constant interference. Freud discovers not simply that the act subverts knowledge, but also that it is precisely from the *breach in knowledge* (the break in the constative) that the act takes its performative *power*: it is the very *knowledge that cannot know itself*,[23] that, in man, *acts*. If subjectivity is henceforth a cognitive (constative) struggle to overcome a series of performative "infelicities," the problem of the analytic *cure* becomes the following: how can "statements" [*constats*] (a recrudescence of knowledge) be transformed *into acts*? How can cognitive recrudescence be transformed into performative profit? For psychoanalysis, like the performative, is above all a quest for happiness: a quest for the *felicity* of acts.

[22]Cf. Paul de Man, "The Purloined Ribbon," in *Glyph*, no. 1 (1977), p. 45, and Shoshana Felman, *La Folie et la chose littéraire* (Paris: Seuil, 1978), p. 24.

[23]This is how Lacan defines the unconscious: "a knowledge that does not allow one to know one knows" (unpublished lecture, 19 February, 1974).

The Subject (of the) Unconscious,
or the Miner's Lamp

Beyond these theoretical coincidences (concepts of referent and act) between the science of the unconscious and that
of the performative, is it possible to characterize Austin's
attitude toward psychoanalysis, concretely and directly?

In his article on "excuses," Austin recommends to philosophers of language, in a general way, that they draw upon
three sorts of "reference books" or "source-books": (1) the
dictionary, that is, the analysis of speech acts (in particular,
acts of excusing or excuses bearing upon acts) on the basis of
ordinary language and everyday usage; (2) law books, that is,
the analysis of legal cases studied in relation to a *judgment*
or a *decision*—"*cases . . . brought up* for decision" (*PP*,
p. 186)—and of "black-and-white decision: guilty or not
guilty" (*PP*, p. 188); (3) finally, "psychology"—the study,
Austin suggests, of "*cases . . . unpressed for decision*" (*PP*,
p. 186).

This recommendation on Austin's part deserves attention, not simply because it signals the importance—and the
relevance—of "psychology" for the "analysis"[24] of language, but for the even more interesting reason that it conceives of the essence of what is to be learned, to be drawn
from the study of "psychology," as having to do with the
principle of *indecision* or of *undecidability*,[25] as opposed to
the principle of requiring *decision*, which is that of the Law.

[24]Alongside the theoretical coincidences between psychoanalysis and
performative theory, we may also note the *lexical coincidence* of the term
"analysis" (Fr. *analyse*), which in English (though not normally in French)
is used to characterize the philosophy of language: "analytic philosophy."
In a way that resonates, for me—but that resonates, here again, from a
meeting without meeting, from the reality of the missed encounter between English and French—Austin is designated in English as an "analyst":
one of the best-known and most influential of "analysts."

[25]From the *deferral* of decision (cases . . . *unpressed* for decision), which
is that of vital *complexity*. Cf. Austin's constant insistence on the irre-
ducibility of vital complexity, which philosophers have the responsibility,
indeed, of reducing or of oversimplifying, but which language reveals. See
Sense and Sensibilia (Oxford: Oxford University Press, 1964) chapter 1,

On the basis of this distinction, one can in fact see the relationship between Benveniste's emphasis on the necessary intervention of the Law as the precondition of the speech act—of its legitimacy—and his unwillingness to accept, on the other hand, Austin's *indecision* concerning the precise demarcation between the constative and the performative; Benveniste requires—legitimately—that the distinction be drawn with *decision,* that the opposition be settled and *made law*: that it be established as grammatical law.[26] Benveniste thus finds himself on the side of the realm of Law and of the teaching of decisiveness, whereas Austin's teaching of indecision puts him rather (or, at least, at the same time) on the side of "psychology." So it is—and for this reason—that Austin takes it upon himself to defend the "'jargon' of psychology":

> Finally, the third source-book is psychology. . . . Here I speak with even more trepidation than about the Law. But this is at least clear, that . . . some ways of acting or explanations of the doing of actions, are here noticed and classified which have not been observed or named by ordinary men. . . . There is real danger in contempt for the 'jargon' of psychology . . . when it sets out to supplement and sometimes . . . to supplant, the language of ordinary life. [*PP,* p. 189]

However, this generous and comprehensive attitude, this apprehensive "flirtation" with the "jargon of psychology,"

---

p. 3 ("over-simplification, schematization, and constant obsessive repetition . . . are . . . far too common to be dismissed as an occasional weakness of philosophers"); and the *Cahiers de Royaumont,* p. 333 ("the diversity of the expressions that we may use draws our attention to the extraordinary complexity of the situations in which we are called upon to speak. That is to say that language clarifies life's complexity for us").

[26] It is clear that, generally speaking, the relation of the Law to acts is somewhat different in Benveniste and in Austin. For Benveniste, the performative is generated, above all, by a *decision* of the *Law.* For Austin, on the other hand, as for Don Juan, the performative presupposes the Law, but is generated only on the basis of the *indecision* (or undecidability) of the possibility of *transgressing* the Law.

does not really involve, or does not deeply involve, psycho-analysis. Austin's explicit references to the problematics of the unconscious are few in number and they are essentially episodic or casual, stemming from the sympathetic but distant attitude of a favorably disposed but basically *uncon-cerned* spectator. "I speak as someone foreign—except by hearsay—to the act and to the account of the act," said Oedipus, too.

It is thus all the more striking to observe to what extent Austin's choice of subjects is analytically suggestive, to what extent these subjects—always original and characteristic—are rich in resonances and in analytic implications. Thus the accent on *promising* (with the privileged example of the promise to marry) touches on the problematics of *desire*; the choice of *excuses*, on the other hand, as one of the most "promising" subjects (*PP*, p. 184) points toward an analysis of denegation and of castration, of the subtle and complex problematics of *guilt*:

> When, then, do we 'excuse' conduct . . . ? When are 'excuses' proffered?

> In general, the situation is one where someone is *accused* of having done something which is . . . untoward.

> . . . perhaps he was under somebody's influence . . . ; it may have been partly accidental, or an unintentional slip. [*PP*, pp. 175–176; Austin's emphasis]

> Not every excuse is apt with every verb . . . : and this provides us with one means of introducing some classification into the vast miscellany of 'actions'. If we classify them according to the particular selection of *breakdowns* to which each is liable, this should assign them their places in . . . some model of the machinery of action. [*PP*, p. 180]

Not only do the linguistic *questions* Austin treats always border on analytic questions, but the linguistic *observations* he makes always seem to proceed from an analytic intuition that is not spelled out, such as the observation of the fact that the verb "can" shares with the verb "know" the linguistic anomaly of having no continuous present tense (we can say "I know," "I can," but we cannot say "I am knowing" as we would say "I am walking"), and, more generally, the analysis showing through the "grammar"—or the linguistic behavior—of "can" the permanence of limits and conditions, thus of the human aptitude for fiasco: a demonstration through language of the "traditional beliefs . . . [that] a human ability or power or capacity is inherently liable not to produce success" (*PP*, p. 218). Another linguistic observation that seems to proceed from a psychoanalytical intuition (from a connotation) is the one that consists, for example, in pointing out that the adverb "inadvertently" has no real antonym in English: "We should be asking ourselves such questions as why there is no use for the adverb 'advertently'. . . . Again, there is no use for 'advertently' at the *same* level as 'inadvertently'" (*PP*, pp. 192–193; Austin's emphasis).

If the theory of illocution studies the act in relation to its intentional context, intentionality itself (like that from which arise such expressions, indeed, as "inadvertently," or "unwittingly," "spontaneously," "impulsively" [*PP*, p. 190]) is often studied as stemming rather from a discontinuity or from a break in intention. Intention, for Austin, is scarcely present to itself, scarcely *conscious*:

> Whatever I am doing is being done . . . amidst a background of *circumstances* (including . . . activities by other agents). . . . Furthermore, the doing of it will involve *incidentally* all kinds of minutiae . . . below the level of any intention. . . .
>
> There is a good deal of freedom in 'structuring' the history of someone's activities by means of words like 'intention'. [*PP*, pp. 284–285; Austin's emphasis]
>
> Although we have this notion of my idea of what I'm doing—and indeed we have as a general rule such an idea, as

it were a miner's lamp on our forehead which illuminates always just so far ahead as we go along—it is not to be supposed that there are any precise rules about the extent and degree of the illumination it sheds. The only general rule is that the illumination is always *limited*, and that in several ways. It will never extend indefinitely far ahead. Of course, all that is to follow, or to be done thereafter, is not what I am intending to do, but perhaps consequences or results or effects thereof. [*PP*, p. 284; Austin's emphasis]

One may say that in this fragment Austin theoretically posits the unconscious. However, *consciousness of the unconscious* does not constitute, for Austin, a thesis or a theoretical statement, but rather a sort of *play* of light with shadow.[27] "I have no conception of the world," Lacan says, "but I have a style" ("Le Symptôme," p. 48). For Austin as for Lacan, the import of the unconscious—or of the shadow left by the miner's lamp—is communicated not by a "conception" but, above all, by a *style*.

Erotics and Linguistic Philosophy, or the Feast of Language

A body is that which enjoys itself [*se jouit*]. That which enjoys itself only through incorporating its enjoyment in a signifying manner.

—Lacan, *Encore*

"According to scientific discourse," writes Roland Barthes, "—or a certain discourse of science—knowledge is statement; in writing, it is an act of stating [*une énonciation*]":

[27]Austin himself, during the Royaumont colloquium, defined "artistic language" in these terms: "that shadowy thing," "those obscure borders where light plays with shadow" (*CR*, p. 350).

The statement, the usual object of linguistics, is given as the product of the subject's absence. The act of stating, by exposing the subject's place and energy, even his deficiency (which is not his absence), focuses on the very reality of language, acknowledging that language is an immense halo of implications, of effects, of echoes, of turns, returns, and degrees. . . . Words are no longer conceived illusively as simple instruments; they are cast as projections, explosions, vibrations, devices, flavours. Writing makes knowledge festive.[28]

To read Austin is quite literally to attend a *festival* of knowledge. Research, carried out "joyously," (*CR*, p. 376), is "pleasing" (*HT*, p. 24), "gratifying" (*HT*, p. 10), sometimes "exhilarating" (*PP*, p. 241). Austin is constantly having a good time: "We pride ourselves on having found an *amusing* occupation from which we think we can profit," he said at Royaumont (*CR*, p. 372). But since profit itself is repeatedly called into question, since in the last analysis, knowledge is "unremunerative" (*PP*, p. 25) and theory *does not pay*, does not pay "the wages",[29] the goal of knowledge is above all the *fun* or enjoyment it procures.

> Già la mensa è preparata.
> Voi suonate, amici cari!
> Giacchè spendo i miei danari,
> Io mi voglio divertir.[30]

The utterance of knowledge, no longer constative but performative, is no longer so much the object of contemplation, but of enjoyment. Knowledge, in other words, is no longer what is to be *seen* in a *representation*, a spectacle: it is what is to be *tasted* in a *feast* of language. As Barthes writes:

[28]Roland Barthes, "Lecture," trans. Richard Howard, in *The Oxford Literary Review*, 4 (Autumn 1979), 35.

[29]See above, "Engagement and Wages," and "Breach of Promise."

[30]The famous song from Don Giovanni's banquet, in Mozart's opera (from the Da Ponte libretto): "The table is set. / Make music, dear friends! / Since I am spending my money freely, / I want to have a good time."

Writing is to be found wherever words have flavour (the
French words for *flavour* (*saveur*) and *knowledge* (*savoir*)
have the same Latin root). Curnonski used to say that in
cooking 'things should have the taste of what they are.'
Where knowledge is concerned, things must, if they are to
become what they are, . . . have that ingredient, the salt of
words. It is this taste of words which makes knowledge pro-
found, fecund. [*Lecture*, pp. 35–36]

To read Austin is not simply to attend a linguistic feast, it is
to be repeatedly *invited* to one:

E se ti piace, mangia con me,[31]

says Don Giovanni to Dona Elvira, in Mozart's opera, just
like Molière's Don Juan:

Oh, say, Monsieur Dimanche, will you eat with me? [IV,
iii]

Similarly, Austin constantly invites his reader or his listener to taste the flavor of words or the *savor of knowledge,*
to participate in the *fun,* in the pleasure or the enjoyment of
the feast.

Much, of course, of the *amusement,* and of the instruction,
comes in drawing the coverts of the microglot, in hounding
down the minutiae, and to this I can do no more here than
incite you. But I owe it to the subject to say that it has long
afforded me what philosophy is so often thought, and made,
barren of—the *fun* of discovery, the *pleasures* of co-opera-
tion, and the *satisfaction* of reaching agreement. [*PP*, p. 175]

This is bound to be a little . . . dry to . . . *digest.* . . . I leave
to my readers the real *fun* of applying it in philosophy. [*HT*,
p. 164]

[31]"And if you please, eat with me."

"Is it not," Lacan asks, "this ambiguity (which is what interpretation plays upon) which puts the symptom in a circular relation with the symbolic? . . . Is there a side of linguistics that is treatable as such? It would be the side that is always the one to which an analyst must be sensitive: the *fun*" ("Le Symptôme," p. 59). *Fun*, whose two semantic ingredients are on the one hand *pleasure* and on the other amusement or enjoyment of *play*, can have two implications, or connotations: that of the pleasure of laughter (the pleasure of playing a joke), and that of the pleasure of enjoyment (the pleasure of erotic *play*)—to which the word "fun" can in some cases refer euphemistically, or as understatement.[32] The pleasure of playing, the pleasure of enjoying: a ludic-humorous connotation and/or an erotic connotation.

It goes without saying that that connotation of laughter, or the *fun* of humor, is found everywhere in Austin's style. But what about the libidinal connotation? Can we speak here, as with Don Juan, of the *eroticism* of Austin's language feast?

In fact, through its figures of speech, through the strategy of its resonances and through its ludic energy, the Austinian utterance—eminently libidinal—never ceases to put into play—to put into *action*—in various ways, the sexual, erotic connotation.

First of all, in the erotic play of the performance of teaching, that is, of the invitation to the feast—on the part of one who, like Don Juan, invites not for profit but for pleasure and who, again like Don Juan, does not seek simply to have pleasure but to *give* it to others, to share both the pleasure—and the desire—of language; a teaching that tries thus not to say but to do, and not so much to incite to *knowledge* as to incite to *desire* and to *enjoyment*, and whose relation to the other is above all a relation of incitation and of excitation:

[32]Cf. for example the title of the film *Fun with Dick and Jane*, or the quotations that the *Oxford English Dictionary* offers to illustrate the use of the word "fun": "'Tho' he talk'd much of virtue, his head always run / Upon something or other she found better fun" (Swift, 1727); "Partridge . . . was a great lover of what is called fun" (Fielding, *Tom Jones*, 1749).

To this I can do no more here than *incite you*. [*PP*, p. 175]

> How widespread is infelicity? . . . Well, it seems clear . . .
> that, although *it has excited us* (or *failed to excite us*) in
> connexion with certain acts . . . , infelicity is an ill to which
> *all** acts are heir. . . . [*HT*, p. 18; *Austin's emphasis][33]

Like Don Juan, Austin draws upon a rhetoric of seduction,
a strategy that uses speech acts of solicitation: teaching, like
love, becomes a performance of *promising*, an act of commitment (a *commissive*, an *espousal*) that indeed *engages*
desire and pleasure.

> We could scarcely hope for a more *promising* exercise than
> the study of excuses. [*PP*, p. 184]

> There are also reasons why it is an *attractive* subject *meth-
> odologically*. [*PP*, p. 181]

Austin's teaching is also a teaching of desire: the performance—or the enactment—of a theory of desire that seeks
above all to communicate the desire of the theory.

It is hardly astonishing, then, if the new tools of performative theory substitute for the traditional philosophical criterion of truth the criteria of desire themselves—"satisfaction" or lack of satisfaction, failure or success, "felicity" or
"infelicity."

> To bet is not . . . merely to utter the words 'I bet' . . . : some-
> one might do that all right, and yet we might still not agree
> that he had in fact . . . *succeeded* in betting. To satisfy our-
> selves of this, we have only, for example, to announce our bet
> after the race is over. Besides the uttering of the words of the
> so-called performative, a good many other things have . . . to

[33]These rhetorical connotations so peculiar to Austin, in which utterance, becoming palpable as it were, proves to be precisely *in excess* of the
theoretical statement, are generally lost in the French translation, which is
exclusively preoccupied with rendering the statement and almost embar-
rassed, it would seem, by Austin's "excesses," which it "corrects" or sys-
tematically reduces.

be right if we are to be said to have *happily brought off our action*. What these are we may hope to discover by . . . classifying types of cases in which something *goes wrong** and the act . . . is therefore at least to some extent a *failure*: the utterance is then, we may say, not indeed false but in general *unhappy*. And for this reason we call the doctrine of *the things that can be and go wrong**. . . . the doctrine of the *Infelicities**. . . . I fear, but at the same time of course hope, that these necessary conditions to be *satisfied* will strike you as obvious. [*HT*, pp. 13–14; * Austin's emphasis]

'Performing actions' then, as actions, . . . will be subject to certain whole *dimensions of unsatisfactoriness* to which all actions are subject. . . . [*HT*, p. 21]

Don Juan, too, is concerned with the problematics of "satisfaction," which is *precisely what he does not give,* even though he does give pleasure. "His retreat *cannot satisfy us*," says Don Carlos (v, iii); and Don Juan: "Alas! With all my heart I should like to give you the *satisfaction* you desire; but Heaven is against it . . ." (v, iii). It is precisely because he has not given (and has not had) satisfaction that Don Juan must die: "At last by his death everyone is *satisfied* . . . I am the only one who is unhappy. . . . My wages, my wages, my wages!" (v, vi) To eliminate Don Juan is to eliminate the lack of satisfaction—or nearly so.

Indeed, is it not just this lack of satisfaction—this unsatisfied desire—that is dramatized by the figure of fire, the fire which, after having metaphorically consumed Don Juan during his life ("the disorders . . . to which the *fire* of my blind youth has brought me" [v, iii]), ends up literally killing him? "Oh Heaven! What do I feel! An invisible fire is burning me, . . . and my whole body is becoming a bed of flaming coals!" (v, vi).

Curiously, this "fire"—an incongruous participant at Don Juan's dinner—also appears at Austin's feast of language. The metaphor of fire appears at once in the terminological choices of his theoretical vocabulary (mis-fire), in his choice of examples, and even at the very heart of his abstractly speculative reflection. Now might not this rhetorical predilection for the figure of fire refer back, here again, as in Molière's play, to a problematics of desire and of its *hold* on reality, to a (metaphoric) thought of the (performative) referential effects of the (speech) act or of (desire's) fire?

> As I go through life . . . , I in general always have an idea— some idea, my idea, or picture, or notion, or conception—of what I'm up to, what I'm engaged in, what I'm about, or in general 'what I'm doing'. . . . *I* know what I'm doing when I strike the match in the vicinity of the haystack. [PP, p. 283; *Austin's emphasis]

> . . . few excuses get us out of it *completely*: the average excuse . . . gets us only *out of the fire* into the frying pan. [PP p. 177; *Austin's emphasis]

> Notoriously, it is impossible to arrive at . . . an over-simplified metaphysics from the obsession with 'things' and their qualities. In a similar way, less commonly recognized even in these semi-sophisticated times, we fall for the myth of the verb. We treat the expression 'doing an action' . . . as a self-explanatory, ground level description. . . . We scarcely notice even the most patent exceptions or difficulties . . . any more than we fret, in the *ivresse des grandes profondeurs*, as to *whether flames are things or events*. [PP, pp. 178–179; *Austin's French]

Thus Austin is in a way like Heraclitus, someone who thinks about fire, thinks about *the undecidability between things and events*. Now, precisely in this undecidability is located the concept of the performative, the conceptual novelty of those events of desire called speech acts—which do "things" with "words" and through which symbolic fire *takes*, in the real.[34]

[34]Cf. my commentary on the Lacanian and Freudian analyses of the dream of fire reported by Freud (at the beginning of Chapter VII of *The Interpretation of Dreams*) in *La Folie et la chose littéraire*, pp. 234–236.

The Last Word of Scandal

If the performative, in fact, is an event—a ritual—of desire, should we be surprised to learn that performative desire always takes as its model, rhetorically, the symbolics of sexual desire? It is not only in the Don Juan myth, it is in Austin that the speech act is modeled on a metaphorics of the "performance"[35] of the sexual act.

It begins with the fact (with the fun of the fact) that the first example of speech act Austin proposes (playfully) is that of marriage.[36] Now in explaining the performative by the effective performance of an act (as opposed to the simple statement/description of the act), Austin has fun equivocating as to the consummate "act" that specifically "accomplishes" a marriage; by equivocating in this way he manages to evoke—with all the greater resonance (and all the more fun)—the *dimension of pleasure that is inherent in the act*:

> . . . the uttering of the sentence is . . . the doing of an action. . . .

> This is far from being as paradoxical as it may sound or as I have *meanly* been *trying to make it sound.* . . .
> Examples:
> (E. *a*) 'I do (sc. take this woman to be my lawful wedded wife)'—as uttered in the course of the marriage ceremony . . . to utter the sentence . . . is not to *describe** my doing . . . : it is to do it. . . .

[35]Sexual "performance," of course, constitutes one important connotation of the word "performance" in English; cf. the fashionable concept of "performance anxiety."

[36]In marriage ceremonies based upon that of the Church of England the correct response is actually "I will," not "I do." However, "I do" is a common misrendering, and it is of course a particularly fitting example of a speech act. The editor of *How to Do Things with Words* notes that "Austin realized that the expression 'I do' is not used in the marriage ceremony too late to correct his mistake. We have let it remain in the text as it is philosophically unimportant that it is a mistake" (p. 5, n. 2).

When I say before the registrar or altar, &c., 'I do,' *I am not reporting on a marriage: I am indulging in it.* [*HT*, pp. 5–6; *Austin's emphasis]

It is by playing in this way on implicit sexual content or erotic resonance that Austin brings into relief the dimension of pleasure that specifies the act as such. What is more, by using a rhetoric of *first person* examples ("I am not reporting on a marriage: I am indulging in it"), Austin's theoretical performance blends with the speech act, participates in both the *doing* and the *enjoying* of the act. Once again, by putting his own theory into action, Austin plays on, and takes pleasure from, the Donjuanian "confusion between meaning and reference"—a licentious confusion that he produces for both the theoretical *seduction* and the theoretical *education* of the reader.

The play on the example of marriage is pursued throughout a major portion of the book which, drawing out the pleasure of the example, turns it into a "prolonged metaphor." Now the implicit sexual content, the ambiguity of the "performance" or "act" that marriage is supposed to "accomplish" only increases when Austin gets to the point of examining the conditions of the "unhappiness" of the act, its "infelicities."

When the utterance is a *misfire* . . . our *act* (marrying &c.) is void or *without effect.* . . . On the other hand, [in cases of *"abuse"*] we speak of our infelicitous act as . . . not implemented, or *not consummated,* rather than as void or without effect. . . .

Two final words about being void or without effect. This does not mean, of course, to say that we won't have done anything: lots of things will have been done—we shall most interestingly have committed the act of bigamy—but we shall *not** have done the purported act, viz marrying. Because despite the name, you do not when bigamous marry twice. (In short, the algebra of marriage is BOOLEAN). [*HT*, pp. 16–17; *Austin's emphasis]

Boolean algebra, or set theory, is thus substituted, in Austin's case, for Don Juan's arithmetic ("Two and two are four, Sganarelle") in a comment, here again, on the very principle of bigamy, of the lacks or "infelicities" of the marriage performance.

Thus it is especially with respect to failures, with respect to fiascos of performance, that Austin's play on the sexual connotation is evident:

> We shall call in general those infelicities . . . which are such that *the act . . . is not achieved,* by the name *MISFIRES:* and on the other hand we may christen those infelicities where the act *is* achieved ABUSES (do not stress the normal connotations of these names!).* [*HT*, p. 16; *Austin's emphasis]

Now if it is especially the *fiascos* of performance that spring from the sexual connotation, is it not because Austinian rhetoric (its "force of utterance") here again, suggestively, rejoins Freudian teaching? Lacan insists that

> Freud's so-called sexuality consists in noting that everything having to do with sex is always a failure. It is the basis and the principle of the very idea of fiasco. *Failure (misfire) itself can be defined as what is sexual in every human act.* That is why there are so many *actes manqués.* Freud indicated perfectly clearly that an *acte manqué* always has to do with sex. The *acte manqué par excellence* is precisely the sexual act. . . . And that is what people are always talking about. ["Le Symptôme," p. 19]

Thus, like Austin, Lacan (after Freud) repeats the Donjuanian scandal. If the problem of the Don Juan myth is in fact the problem of the relation of the erotic and the linguistic, the scandal lies not so much in the fact that the linguistic is always erotic, but in the much more scandalous fact that the erotic is always linguistic. In other words, the scandal lies less in sex than in language, insofar as language is inhabited by the *act of failing* through which the body is lacking to itself: the act of failing through which the body's *doing* always fails to speak itself, whereas the *speaking* never fails to *do*. If, then, as Lacan says, "language, whatever it may be, is an obscenity" ("Vers un signifiant nouveau," p. 12), it is not so much because the speech act always connotes the sexual act, but rather because the human sexual act always connotes the speech act—the act *par excellence* of the speaking body, which subsists only insofar as it speaks, and which cannot know whether it, or the fire that it carries, is after all really a "thing" or only an "event." Does not Don Juan in a way raise the following troubling question: When the speaking body *does* something ("makes love," for example), what sort of "doing" is involved? Does he not suggest (like Austin, like Freud, like Lacan) that most scandalous of all propositions: The sexual act, in the speaking being, might be only a speech act . . . ? "There is no sexual relation," says Lacan, speaking aphoristically; there is *relation* with the Other only through "the intermediary of that which *makes sense in language.*"[37] And Austin:

> 'To marry is, in some cases, simply to say a few words.' [*HT*, p. 8]

> And *the act of marrying, like, say, the act of betting,* is at least *preferably** . . . to be described as *saying certain words,** rather than as performing a different, inward and spiritual, action. [*HT*, p. 13; *Austin's emphasis]

Thus Austin, like Don Juan, reveals the erotic scandal of linguistic philosophy—the incongruous interdependence of the failed operations of sex and language.

Failure, to be sure, pervades every performance, including even that of theory, which in turn becomes erotic for being nothing but a failed act, or an act of failing. Austin himself, as we have seen, can only fail in his own act, fail to keep his own *promise* to *say* the constative of the performative. Far from achieving the satisfaction of theoretical "felicity," the

[37]Unpublished lecture, 11 June 1974.

Austinian performance is itself exposed to *misfire*: "On this point I could do no more than explode a few hopeful fireworks" (*HT*, p. 148).

Now if Austin finds himself indeed, as he says, impassioned, "excited" by infelicity (*HT*, p. 18), it is not because he likes to fail, or takes pleasure in misfiring, but because the pleasure of the feast surpasses the simple success or achievement of performance, because in a certain way the fun—the pleasure of linguistic *doing*—goes well beyond the "happiness" of language or the "felicity" of the act. There exists, in fact, in Austin, something like a *pleasure in scandal*, a performative pleasure if ever there was one, which is inherent in the act but is not necessarily confused with its achievement; an insidious pleasure, whose scandalous rhetoric carries the theoretical suspicion that every act may be—as act—nothing other than the very event of such a scandal, and the very advent of such a pleasure.

Beyond the Felicity Principle: The Performance of Humor

In the eyes of one who has all knowledge and all power, the comic does not exist.
—Baudelaire, "On the Essence of Laughter"

Alice said rather impatiently: "I don't belong to this railway journey at all—I was in a wood just now—and I wish I could get back there!"

"You might make a joke on that," said the little voice close to her ear: "something about 'you would if you could,' you know."

"Don't tease so," said Alice, looking about in vain to see where the voice came from. "If you're so anxious to have a joke made, why don't you make one yourself?"

The little voice sighed deeply. It was *very* unhappy, evidently. . . .
    —Lewis Carroll, *Through the Looking-Glass*

The act of *failing* thus leads, paradoxically, to an *excess* of
utterance: manifest through its pleasure, independent of the
"felicity" of its search for knowledge, the Austinian "force
of utterance" is constantly in excess over the *meaning* of the
theoretical statement. It is precisely this excess of energy
that is continually discharged through humor. "[Some]
French authors," writes Freud, "describe laughter as a 'dé-
tente'. . . . We should say that laughter arises if a quota of
psychical energy . . . has become unusable, so that it can
find free discharge."[38]
Humor indeed is preeminently not a "saying" but a
"doing": a "making (someone) laugh." If Austin is continually taking and giving the pleasure of jokes, it is because, paradoxically, the supreme performance of the *body's*
failing itself is that of making jokes [*faire de l'esprit*].
To be sure, the "joke" participates in the "doing" of seduction, stemming in its turn, like the banquet Don Juan
offers, from the gratuitousness of the gift of pleasure. As
Freud writes, "the psychical process in the hearer . . . can
scarcely be more aptly described than by stressing the fact
that he has bought the pleasure of the joke with very small
expenditure on his own part. *He might be said to have been
presented with it*" (*Jokes*, p. 148). However, Austin's invitation to laughter is not just (yet another) invitation to pleasure but, more specifically, an invitation to the *pleasure of
scandal*: "we shall most interestingly," as Austin put it,
"have committed the act of bigamy." The laughter pro-
voked by a joke turns the reader into an *accomplice*: an
accomplice precisely in scandal. As Freud writes: "I am

[38]Sigmund Freud, *Jokes and Their Relation to the Unconscious*, trans.
James Strachey (New York: Norton, 1960), p. 147. This work will hereafter
be designated *Jokes*.

merely a listener who has not assisted in this functioning of [the criminal's] sense of humor, but I feel its effect, as it were from a distance. I detect in myself a certain humorous satisfaction, possibly much as he does."[39]

Scandal, of course, is never thematized or articulated, never explicitly denoted; it is nonetheless insidiously connoted by the oblique, always maliciously aberrant insistence on the humor—the incongruous humor—of *examples*. Consider, for example, the humor of scandal or the scandal of humor in the following examples, which are quite characteristic of Austin's style:

Examples of intentionality:

> Suppose I tie a string across a stairhead. A fragile relative, from whom I have expectations, trips over it, falls, and perishes. Should we ask whether I tied the string there intentionally? Well, but it's hard to see how I could have done such a thing unintentionally. . . . You don't do that sort of thing—by accident? By mistake? Inadvertently? On the other hand, would I be bound to admit I did it 'on purpose' . . . ? That has an ugly sound. What could the purpose have been if not to trip at least someone? Maybe I had better claim I was simply passing the time . . . practising tying knots. [*PP*, pp. 274–275]

Examples of excuses:

> We may plead that we trod on the snail inadvertently: but not on a baby—you ought to look where you are putting your great feet. [*PP*, p. 194]

Examples of infelicities:

> Suppose, for example, I see a vessel on the stocks, walk up and smash the bottle hung at the stem, proclaim 'I name this ship the *Mr. Stalin*'. . . : but the trouble is, I was not the person chosen to name it (whether or not—an additional

[39]Sigmund Freud, "Humour" (1928), in *Character and Culture* (New York: Collier Books, 1963), pp. 263–264.

complication—*Mr. Stalin* was the destined name; perhaps in a way it is even more of a shame if it was). We can all agree:
1) that the ship was not thereby named;
2) that it is an infernal shame.
. . . It is a mockery, like a marriage with a monkey. [*HT*, pp. 23–24]

When the saint baptized the penguins, was this void because the procedure of baptizing is inappropriate to be applied to penguins, or because there is no accepted procedure of baptizing anything except humans? [*HT*, p. 24]

What makes us laugh, in the examples, is the unexpectedness of their at once incongruous and trivial character, which brings to mind the figures of speech and the rhetorical strategies of the heroï-comic genre, in which the comic is based, in fact, on the incongruous mix of the sublime and the ridiculous. "Laughter" Baudelaire writes, "is essentially contradictory; that is to say that it is at once a token of an infinite grandeur and an infinite misery. . . . It is from the perpetual collision of these two infinites that laughter is struck."[40] Consider, again, in Austin, the following example (of an excuse) which, using the most characteristic of the heroï-comic figures,[41] might well be one of Don Juan's remarks, so well does it reflect a lucid view of the inherent incongruity of the speaking body:

If I have broken your dish or your romance, maybe the best defence I can find will be clumsiness. [*PP*, p. 177]

"Laughter," writes Freud, quoting Herbert Spencer, "naturally results only when consciousness is unawares transferred from great things to small—only when there is what

[40] Baudelaire, "On the Essence of Laughter," in *The Mirror of Art*, trans. Jonathan Mayne (London: Phaidon Press, 1955), p. 141; hereafter designated "Laughter."
[41] This figure of speech is called *zeugma* ("yoking"). Cf. the famous example of it (and of its heroï-comic effect) in Pope, *The Rape of the Lock:* "Here thou, great Anna! whom three realms obey / Dost sometimes counsel take—and sometimes Tea."

we may call a *descending* incongruity" (*Jokes*, p. 146). Through the shock effect of the laughter that it provokes, the descending incongruity of Austin's examples seems to institute, as it were, triviality itself as a philosophy—as a method.[42]

> The more we imagine the situation in detail, with a *background of story*—and it is worth employing *the most idiosyncratic* . . . means to stimulate and to discipline our wretched imaginations—the less we find we disagree about what we should say. [*PP*, p. 184]

Austin's "example" is thus a "story," a case history—and the case is "idiosyncratic," trivially and derisorily incongruous. Now what is trivial is only what is peripheral to the center: to the center of (conscious) attention. Austin's humor in his choice of examples thus produces, in the theoretical space, a decentering effect that we may call analytic.

In general, the relation of Austin's methodical "philosophy" of language to the triviality of his "examples" is strangely like the relation of psychoanalytic theory to the vulgarity of "case histories." With Austin as with psychoanalysis, the irreducible triviality of the idiosyncratic is that of a *practice* of the singular.

Of a practice, that is, of what belongs to the order of *doing*. For unlike saying, doing is always trivial: it is that which, by definition, cannot be generalized. As Benveniste says with respect to the performative, the act "has the property of being *unique*. It cannot be produced except in special circumstances, at one and only one time, at a definite date and place. It does not have the value of definition or prescription but, once again, of performance. This is why it is often ac-

---

[42]Cf. the *credo* of the later Wittgenstein (one of the major influences on analytic philosophy), who used to say that philosophy would have no future except to become become (like aesthetics, and like ethics) a "synopsis of trivia." See G. E. Moore, "Wittgenstein's Lectures in 1930–1933," in *Classics of Analytic Philosophy*, ed. R. R. Ammerman (New York: McGraw-Hill, 1965), p. 284.

companied by indications of date, of place, of names of people, witnesses, etc." (p. 236). Thus true History, belonging to the order of acts or of practice, is always—however grandiose it may be—made up of trivialities.

The same is true of writing. Barthes writes:

> A writer—by which I mean . . . the subject of a praxis—
> must have the persistence of the watcher who stands at the
> crossroads of all other discourses, in a position that is *trivial*
> in respect to purity of doctrine (*trivialis* is the etymological
> attribute of the prostitute who waits at the intersection of
> three roads). ["Lecture," p. 37; Barthes's emphasis]

Now at the intersection of three paths it is not simply the prostitute—or sex, always illicit—that is waiting or that one is meeting, but also the murder of the father—of Laius, still unknown. Hence a murder that is, literally and in every sense of the words, peripheral and trivial.

Indeed, however trivial it may be, the often black humor of Austin's examples abounds in images of murders and of monstrous marriages ("marriage with a monkey," "bigamy," etc.). The triviality of the witty example is thus incongruous only because it belongs to a radically heteronomous space, because it brings about the intervention, on the homogeneous plane of the theoretical stage, the heroï-comic heterogeneity of the *Other Stage*.

*

Thus there exists, in Austin's text, a *disparity of levels* between the theoretical statement and the presence—which is all the more pronounced in that it is incongruous—of that Other Stage, a disparity of levels between theory and humor, between meaning and pleasure. Now the passage from one level to another is not harmonious, gradual, continuous; on the contrary, it is—like laughter—convulsive and brutal. Meaning, in fact, can be accompanied by pleasure only on condition that it *fall* from one level to another. In other words, the passage from one textual plane to another is on the order of a skid or a fall.

Now the fall is the supreme example of what provokes laughter. "What is there," Baudelaire asks, "so delightful in the sight of a man falling on the ice or in the street, or stumbling at the end of a pavement?" ("Laughter," p. 139).

> SGANARELLE: My reasoning is that there is something admirable in man, whatever you may say. . . . Isn't it wonderful that I am here, and that I have something in my head that thinks . . . and makes my body do whatever it wants. . . ? (*He drops dizzily to the ground.*)
> DON JUAN: There! Your reasoning has fallen flat on its face! [III, i]

Austin's humor is the humor of the fall—a humor that is closely tied to the performative, since falling is an *act: the* act, indeed, in so far as it is a failure—the very prototype of the *acte manqué.* In English, moreover, a "lapsus" is commonly called a "slip," a "slip of the tongue."

Indeed Austin, like a good skier, delights in slides and slips—and his awareness of them, as his vocabulary attests, is very highly developed:

> It's very easy to *slip* into this view. [*PP*, p. 236]

> We have discussed the performative utterance and its infelicities. That equips us . . . with two *shining new skids* under our metaphysical feet. [*PP*, p. 241]

> It is a matter of unpicking, one by one, a mass of *seductive* (mainly verbal) fallacies. . . . We may hope to learn something . . . about the meanings of some English words . . . philosophically *very slippery.*[43]

What is dangerously "slippery" is thus seduction itself ("a mass of seductive fallacies"); what *causes skidding,* in lan-

---

[43]Austin, *Sense and Sensibilia,* pp. 4–5.

guage, is especially pleasure itself, inasmuch as it surreptitiously causes one to slide—without being aware of it—outside the realm of meaning, outside the terrain of knowledge.

"Vainly I strive against it," writes Kierkegaard. "My foot slips. My life is still a poet's existence."[44] The seduction of slipping is thus the seduction of poetry, of the *poetic* functioning of language. "Stumbling over words like cobblestones" is, in one of Baudelaire's definitions, the nature of the poetic act.[45] The Austinian performance thus participates, in a way, in poetic performance.

Now if to give pleasure (poetic or humorous) is to seduce or to lead the reader—unbeknowst to himself—onto essentially *slippery* ground, the performance of humor, or the act accomplished by a joke, is not simply the act of provoking laughter, but also that of tripping. "What could the purpose have been if not to trip at least someone?" Austin asked in his insidiously oblique fashion, playing on his favorite rhetoric of first-person "examples": "Maybe I had better claim I was simply passing the time, playing . . . , practising tying knots" (*PP*, p. 275). Tripping someone, however, is obviously much more than a "pastime": it is not simply a *pleasurable* act, it is also, and especially, a *subversive* act.

In fact, humor in Austin intervenes very often only to subvert knowledge, to call it into question, to cast doubt upon it. For Baudelaire, "laughter is only an expression, a symptom, a diagnostic. Symptom of what? That is the question" ("Laughter," p. 143). "We do not know," Freud says, similarly, "what is giving us enjoyment and what we are laughing at. This uncertainty in our judgment, which must be assumed to be a fact, may have provided the motive for the construction of jokes in the proper sense of the word" (*Jokes*, p. 132). Pleasure is pleasure only in not knowing

[44]Søren Kierkegaard, *Either/Or*, vol. I, trans. D. F. Swenson and L. M. Swenson (Garden City: Doubleday, 1959), p. 35.

[45]"I venture out alone to drill myself / In what must seem an eerie fencing-match /Duelling in dark corners for a rhyme / *And stumbling over words like cobblestones* / Where now and then realities collide / With lines I dreamed of writing long ago" (Baudelaire, "The Sun," in *Les Fleurs du Mal*, trans. Richard Howard (Boston: Godine, 1982), p. 88.

where it comes from; the comic is comic only in that it does not know its own nature.[46] Jokes achieve, in this way, an unsettling effect with respect to knowledge: according to Freud, "they [set] themselves up against . . . critical judgment" (*Jokes*, p. 133). The entire effort of the Austinian enterprise of performative theory is directed at subverting the *cognitive evidence* inherent in the constative. This general problematization of the presumption of "knowing" is constantly enacted through the nervous energy of humor:

> Of course philosophers have been wont to talk as though you or I or anybody could just go round stating anything about anything and that would be perfectly in order, only there's just a little question: is it true or false? But besides the little question, is it true or false, there is surely the question: *is* it in order? Can you go round just making statements about anything? Suppose for example you say to me, 'I'm feeling pretty mouldy this morning.' Well, I say to you, 'You're not,' and you say 'what the devil do you mean, I'm not?' I say, 'Oh, nothing—I'm just stating you're not, is it true or false?' And you say, 'Wait a bit about whether it's true or false, the question is what did you mean by making statements about somebody else's feelings? I told you I'm feeling pretty mouldy. You're just not in a position to say, to state that I'm not.' This brings out that you can't just make statements about other people's feelings (though you can make guesses if you like); and there are very many things which, having no knowledge of, not being in a position to pronounce about, you just can't state. [*PP*, p. 249]

Still, humor constitutes not only an assault on knowledge but also an assault on power, on repression in every sense of the word—political or analytical. Freud explains:

> The main characteristic of the joke-work [is] that of liberating pleasure by *getting rid of inhibitions*. . . . [The power of

[46]"Artists . . . know that such-and-such a being is comic, and that it is so only on condition of its being unaware of its nature" (Baudelaire, "Laughter," p. 153).

jokes] lies in the yield of pleasure which they draw from the sources of play upon words and of liberated nonsense. [*Jokes,* p. 134]

An examination of the determinants of laughing will perhaps lead us to a plainer idea of what happens when a joke affords assistance against suppression. [*Jokes,* p. 136]

In fact, the Austinian performance of humorous *slipping* aims above all at shaking the institution of prejudice itself, the institution of beliefs or received ideas: "To feel the firm ground of prejudice slipping away is exhilarating . . ." (*HT,* p. 61). Thus the act of provoking laughter (of provoking pleasure), by causing a slip (by tripping) leads to the act of *exploding.* If laughter is, literally, a sort of explosion of the speaking body, the act of exploding—with laughter—becomes an explosive performance in every sense of the word.

What we need to do for the case of stating, and by the same token describing and reporting, is to *take them a bit off their pedestal.* [*PP,* pp. 249–250]

I distinguish five very general classes. . . . They are . . . quite enough to *play Old Harry with two fetishes* which I admit to an inclination to play Old Harry with, viz. (1) the true/false fetish, (2) the value/fact fetish. [*HT,* p. 151]

The subversive performance of laughter rejoins the performance—a supremely Donjuanian performance—of the iconoclast. Like Don Juan, Austin takes pleasure—to use his own terms—in *playing Old Harry,* playing the devil.[47] The comic, as Baudelaire, too, says, is "of diabolic origin" ("Laughter," p. 137).

Now to "play the devil" is above all to renounce playing God; that means—in Don Juan's fashion—not believing in the promise of Heaven as the power that underwrites the

[47]Cf. Claude Reichler's highly suggestive book, *La Diabolie* (Paris: Minuit, 1979).

promising animal; not believing, by the same token, in the promise of the promising animal, even if that animal is himself.

If Austin, like Don Juan, is constantly making promises in order not to keep them, this self-subversion of his own promise is achieved—through humor—at the very outset, in the witty play of his titles. If Austin's humor, as a whole, has managed to go unnoticed by commentators and inter-preters, who have never *taken it into consideration,* it is nevertheless surprising to see to what an extent the world of theory has managed to remain blind to the fact that Austin's titles are, above all, jokes.

How to Do Things with Words exploits in an ironically witty fashion the conventional formula of how-to manuals, of practical guides: "How to Make Money," "How to Make Love," "How to Repair your House," or, better still, *How to Win Friends and Influence People, How to Stop Worrying and Start Living.*[48] How to do things with words: practical recipes for the speaking body: "everything you need to *know* in order to *be able* . . ."; *scilicet*—"you can know" (when you have read this book) how to do this with words; nothing is simpler, nothing easier. . . . The pernicious humor of the title is directed against its author, against his *promise of teaching*: it suggests, by antiphrasis, that we are perhaps dealing here with the *unteachable,* with the non-cognitive, with the heteronomy of "things."

Or another famous title: "A Plea for Excuses," which might be paraphrased "an excuse for excuses." When Austin was being questioned at Royaumont on the necessity for types of research other than his own (psychological research, for example), he, as usual, responded with a joke:

> I favor that sort of research, and I can only refer you to an article of mine in which I have formulated my credo on this point: an article very aptly entitled "Excuses"; since my

[48]These latter two popular titles are both by Dale Carnegie (New York: Pocket Books, 1st ed., 1936).

credo amounts in the end to excusing myself for not doing what I have no intention of doing. [*CR*, p. 375]

"A Plea for Excuses" begins with a play on its title:

> The subject of this paper, *Excuses*, is one not to be treated, but only to be introduced, within such limits. . . . What, then, is the subject? I am here using the word 'excuses' *for a title*, but it would be unwise to freeze too fast to this one noun . . . The field . . . includes 'plea,' 'defence,' 'justification' and so on. [*PP*, p. 175; Austin's emphasis]

"I am . . . using the word 'excuses' *for a title*": this may mean either that "the word 'excuses' indeed appears in the title of this essay," or "I am speaking under this title, by way of excuse"; thus it may mean either "the noun 'excuse' is what I am talking about"; or "I am speaking *in the name of excuses.*" Thus Austin's self-subverting humor manages from the outset to enact the subject of excuses: I am introducing, says Austin, the (new) subject of excuses; although this subject has been neglected up to now, I find it very important, it deserves an apology, a defense; I am thus about to excuse (or justify) excuses; I apologize, however, for being unable to do it in a satisfactory way within the limits of this essay; thus I am excusing excuses; but I excuse myself for failing to excuse them as I ought.

Perhaps the richest title, the one whose humor is most subtle and most sophisticated, is "Three Ways of Spilling Ink," the title of a study presented as a lecture in a colloquium entitled "Responsibility" organized by the American Society of Political and Legal Philosophy. "Three Ways of Spilling Ink" takes on the study of three ways of expressing intention in English: "intentionally," "deliberately," and "on purpose." Austin's title, in the context of "political and legal philosophy," seems somewhat irreverent; but we quickly discover that the title "merely" alludes to an *example* in the text, an example Austin uses to get his study off the ground. The triviality of his title is thus explained—at least apparently—by the triviality of the example.

> A schoolteacher may ask a child who has spilled the ink in class: 'Did you do that intentionally?' or 'Did you do that deliberately?' or 'Did you do that on purpose. . . ?' They appear to mean the same. But do they really? [*PP*, p. 274]

> Let us distinguish between acting *intentionally* and acting *deliberately* or *on purpose*, as far as this can be done by attending to what language can teach us. [*PP*, p. 273]

Given the example of the child, the "three ways"—the three accredited ways—of "spilling ink" may have a double meaning: they are either the three ways in which the child carries out the action of spilling the ink—*three ways of acting* designated by the three expressions of intention; or *three linguistic ways* of *speaking* of the child's act, of describing its intentionality; in this latter case, it is Austin himself who is the ink-spiller, as he studies the three expressions and *writes his article* on the child's "three ways." The humorous play of the title thus suggests that writing itself (in this case, Austin's writing on the theory of language or of acts) is in some way of the same order of "responsibility" or of intentionality as the child's play or as his act (pleasure-seeking? insolent? gratuitous?—in any case, enigmatic) of spilling ink.

Humor, as Freud rightly says, goes back to the pleasure—again, an "irresponsible" pleasure—of child's play. Beginning with a reference to Bergson's *Le Rire*, Freud stresses the fact that Bergson

> endeavours to explain the comic as an after-effect of the joys of childhood. 'Peut-être même devrions-nous . . . chercher dans les jeux qui amusèrent l'enfant la première ébauche des combinaisons qui font rire l'homme . . . Trop souvent surtout nous méconnaissons ce qu'il y a d'encore enfantin, pour ainsi dire, dans la plupart de nos émotions joyeuses.' (Bergson, 1900, 68ff.)[49] Since we have traced back jokes to chil-

---

[49]'Perhaps we should even carry simplification further still, go back to our oldest memories, and trace in the games that amused the child the first sketch of the combinations which make the grown man laugh. . . . Above all, we too often fail to recognize how much of childishness, so to speak, there still is in most of our joyful emotions' (*Jokes*, p. 223, n. 1).

dren's play with words and thoughts which has been frustrated by rational criticism . . . we cannot help feeling tempted to investigate the infantile roots . . . in the case of the comic as well. . . . Children themselves do not strike us as in any way comic, though their own nature fulfils all the conditions which, if we compare it with our own nature, yield a comic difference. . . . A child only produces a comic effect on us when he conducts himself not as a child but as a serious adult. . . . But so long as he retains his childish nature the perception of him affords us a pure pleasure, perhaps one that reminds us slightly of the comic. We call him naive, in so far as he shows us his lack of inhibition, and we describe as naively comic those of his utterances which in another person we should have judged obscenities or jokes. [*Jokes*, pp. 222–223]

"Three ways of spilling ink," Austin's title said, putting on an equal footing—through its malicious humor—the child's activity and that of the philosopher-writer who is studying, in fact, the intentionality of this activity. Austin's text never *answers* the question "why did the child spill ink?" It only enumerates, inventories the variety of possible questions—a list that one might be tempted to prolong: Did the child spill the ink maliciously? spitefully? just for fun? or simply because he was clumsy? We shall never know. The schoolteacher's questions are doomed to remain unanswered.

> A schoolteacher may ask a child who has spilled the ink in class: 'Did you do that intentionally?' or 'Did you do that deliberately?' or 'Did you do that on purpose (or purposely)?'

"Why do you spill ink?" Austin was asked—in another style—at Royaumont.

> So, to go back to the questions which seemed to be addressed more particularly to me. . . . We are dealing once again with the method of analytic philosophy. We are asked why we are doing what we are trying to do when we behave as we do. When I am asked this question, I find myself rather in the position of one of my colleagues who had some children and, whenever he was about to punish one of them, was

restrained by the fact that he couldn't manage to remember any of the reasons one has for punishing children. The same is true for me. When I am asked why I do what I do, I remain silent. [*CR*, p. 348]

"Three ways of spilling ink":

To write—

The inkwell, crystal like a consciousness, with its drop, at the bottom, of darkness . . . sets aside the lamp.

You noticed, one does not write, luminously, on a dark field . . . ; man pursues black on white.

The writer, of his troubles . . . or of a gladness, must make of himself, in the text, the spiritual histrion.[50]

By making ink flow, Austinian humor, as Mallarmé would say, "pursues black on white," and making of itself, in the text, the spiritual histrion, *sets aside the lamp.*

"How to do things with words," "a plea for excuses," "three ways of spilling ink": what Austin's titles do, through humor, is to suspend their own entitlement—their own authority. The titles, as titles, are promises (promises of new subjects, promises of authorial authority, promises of knowing or learning: "How to do . . ."; "we could scarcely hope for a more promising exercise than the study of excuses" [*PP*, p. 184])—and, at the same time, in the same breath, the titles call into question their own right to promise, subvert their own promise. This amounts to saying that the titles, drops of spilled ink, only *do* something—with wit—by suspending their own authority to *say* something.

"The man who trips," writes Baudelaire, "would be the last to laugh at his own fall, unless he happened to be a philosopher, one who had acquired by habit a power of rapid self-division and thus of assisting as a disinterested specta-

---

[50]Mallarmé, "L'Action restreinte," in *Oeuvres complètes*, p. 370.

tor at the phenomena of his own *ego*" ("Laughter," p. 141).
Austin in fact never leaves off laughing at his own fall, never
ceases to make a *philosophic joke* of the performance of his
own slipping:

> So far then we have merely felt the firm ground of prejudice
> slide away beneath our feet. But now how, as *philosophers,*
> are we to proceed? One thing we might go on to do, of
> course, is to take it all back: another would be to *bog, by
> logical stages, down.* But all this must take time. [*HT*, p. 13]

> (I must explain again that we are floundering here. To feel
> the firm ground of prejudice slipping away is exhilarating,
> but brings its revenges.) [*HT*, p. 61]

Austin's humor stems, in this way, not only from the *subversive* performance inherent in the unconscious, but also
from the *self-subverting* performance inherent in the superego. As Freud writes:

> The joke, it may be said, is the contribution made to the
> comic from the realm of the unconscious. . . . [*Jokes*, p. 208]

> In just the same way, *humor would be a contribution to the
> comic made through the agency of the super-ego. . . .*

> In other respects, we know that the super-ego is a stern
> master. It may be said that it accords ill with its character
> that it should wink at affording the ego a little gratifica-
> tion. . . . The principal thing is the intention which humour
> fulfils, whether it concerns the subject's self or other people.
> Its meaning is: "Look here! This is all that this seemingly
> dangerous world amounts to. Child's play—the very thing to
> jest about!"
> If the super-ego does try to comfort the ego by humour and
> to protect it from suffering, this does not conflict with its
> derivation from the parental function.

> If it is really the super-ego which, in humour, speaks such
> kindly words of comfort to the intimidated ego, this teaches

us that we still have very much to learn about the nature of
that energy. ["Humour," pp. 268–269]

Thus the fun-loving Austin is not simply a man of pleasure,
not simply, either, a man who takes pleasure in laughing; he
is also, and especially, someone who, as a philosopher, takes
pleasure in laughing, above all, *at pleasure,* someone whose
philosophical performance indeed never stops laughing at
its own pleasure. The constitutive relationship of theory
and jokes in Austin's work suggests at every turn that the
apparent convergence of pleasure and rigor is only a decoy
[*leurre*],[51] but at the same time, that "those who are not
duped err."[52] If Austin's Gay Science is finally, as Proust
would say, the science "of that perpetual error that is
known, precisely, as 'life,'" the seductive coincidence between cognitive rigor and performative pleasure points
ceaselessly, through humor, toward its residue:

> In philosophy it is *can** in particular that we seem so often
> to uncover, just when we had thought some problem settled,
> *grinning residually* up at us like the frog at the bottom of the
> beer mug. [*PP*, p. 231; *Austin's emphasis]

The *residual* smile of humor thus makes concrete the theory's problematics of "can" as leaving an irreducible re-
mainder: what, from the theoretical performance—performance of the incongruence between knowledge and
pleasure—emerges as that which is present at once, irreducibly, as *more* and *less* than "felicity."

---

[51]Cf. Paul de Man, "The Epistemology of Metaphor," *Critical Inquiry,* 5
(Fall 1978), 30: "Finally, our argument suggests that the relationship and
the distinction between literature and philosophy cannot be made in terms
of a distinction between aesthetic and epistemological categories. All philosophy is condemned, to the extent that it is dependent upon figuration, to
be literary and, as the depository of this very problem, all literature is to
some extent philosophical. . . . Contrary to common belief, literature is not
the place where the unstable epistemology of metaphor is suspended by
aesthetic pleasure . . . It is rather the place where the possible convergence
of rigor and pleasure is shown to be a delusion."
[52]*Les non-dupes errent.*

What History Cannot Assimilate, or the Stone Feast

The fact of saying remains forgotten behind what is said in what is heard.

—Lacan, "L'Etourdit"

"I'm sure I didn't mean—" Alice was beginning, but the Red Queen interrupted her impatiently.

"That's just what I complain of? You *should* have meant! What do you suppose is the use of a child without any meaning? Even a joke should have a meaning—and a child's more important than a joke, I hope." . . .

"She's in that state of mind," said the White Queen, "that she wants to deny *something*—only she doesn't know what to deny!"

—Lewis Carroll, *Through the Looking-Glass*

Speaking of comedy, Aristotle remarked that "its early stages passed unnoticed, because it was not as yet taken up in a serious way."[53] The same may be said of Austin's humor: the theoretician's enormous influence notwithstanding, his humorous performance has no history, because history has not "taken it seriously." Although it has been influenced by Austin, the history of ideas has not applied his teaching to the effort to understand him or to approach his theory: both the theoretical school derived from Austin and the occasional criticism directed against him have paid attention only to what he *says*, not to what he *does*.

It has thus been possible to criticize Austin for defending the values of "seriousness," to reproach him in particular for his *theoretical* exclusion of joking or play from his philosophy of the performative, on the basis of quotations such as the following:

[53]*De Poetica*, ch. v, 1449a.

'I promise to . . .' Surely the words must be spoken *'seriously'* and so as to be taken *'seriously'*? This is, though vague, true enough in general—it is an important commonplace in discussing the purport of any utterance whatsoever. *I must not be joking,* for example, nor writing a poem. [*HT,* p. 9]

A performative utterance will, for example, be *in a peculiar way***** hollow or void if said by an actor on the stage, or if introduced in a poem, or spoken in soliloquy. This applies in a similar manner to any and every utterance. . . . Language in such circumstances is in special ways—intelligibly—*used not seriously,* but in ways *parasitic***** upon its *normal use*— ways which fall under the doctrine of the *etiolations***** of language. All this we are *excluding***** from consideration. [*HT,* p. 22; *****Austin's emphasis]

It is on the basis of such quotations that Austin is deemed to be caught red-handed defending "seriousness," what is "considered normal," as opposed to the "parasitism," the "unseriousness" of poetry, play, or joking, which thus find themselves excluded.

However, when Austin says, using his favorite first-person rhetoric, "I must not be joking, for example," is it certain that we must—that we may—*believe him*? Coming from a jester like Austin, might not that sentence itself be taken as a denegation—as a joke? Is Austin joking or not, when he says "I must not be joking, for example"? Critics who reproach Austin for excluding jokes, on the basis of the Austinian *statement,* are failing to take into account the Austinian *act,* failing to take into account the close and infinitely complex relationship maintained, throughout Austin's work, between the theory and jokes. What the critics of Austinian "seriousness," of his exclusion of joking, do, paradoxically, is exclude his joking—they fail to take it seriously. We end up here, historically speaking, at the heart of the Aristotelian paradox.

And yet, as we have seen, throughout his indefatigable

humorous performance—which corrodes everything, even his titles—Austin's theory taken as a whole, is presented (perhaps!) as a "joke": one (or several) way(s) to "spill ink."

Now if indeed Austin is clearly *not* a mere champion of the cause of "seriousness," no more is he, in reality (and despite his explicit attack on "seriousness," moreover[54]), a mere champion or defender of "unseriousness." If Austin *dis-plays seriousness*, it is not in order to *play an unserious role* but—in his own words—to *play the devil*. Is the devil "serious" or "unserious"? This is just what it is impossible to *decide*. Theory, which is by definition foreign to humor, is generally speaking in the habit, on the contrary, of playing God: of *underwriting*, by its authority of "supposed knowledge," the values or theses it proposes. But with Austin, there are in fact no more guarantees, no more for "unseriousness" than for "seriousness": the discourse of the "unserious" does not *take*, it slips or slides away with all the rest. The devil, in other words, does not take himself for God. With Austin, at the very least, the devil's chief characteristic is precisely that he *does not know* whether he is playing seriously or not, whether he is or is not in the process of playing or joking. That is the truly diabolical question inherent in joking, or in play: *Is* it a joke? *Is* it simply a game? The distinguishing feature of the Austinian performance is not that it turns "seriousness" against "unseriousness," but rather that it *blurs* the boundaries between the two.

Now it is just this play of undecidability promoted by *diabolical* humor that the history of ideas—or the history of Austin's influence—proves not to have retained, not to have been able to "digest," to incorporate, or to assimilate. In fact, it is not only the eminently critical "continental"

---

[54]See, for example, *How to Do Things with Words*, p. 10: "It is gratifying to observe in this very example how excess of profundity, or rather solemnity, at once paves the way for immorality." And, similarly, *Philosophical Papers*, p. 271: "What, finally, is the importance of all this . . . ? I will answer this shortly, although *I am not sure importance is important*: truth is."

reception[55] but also the eminently admiring and accepting Anglo-Saxon one which in turn have *missed* Austin's "devil-playing," have failed to grasp the purport of his humorous performance. The most important American philosophers of language who consider themselves Austin's "heirs"[56] completely miss the Austinian blurring of the "serious" and the "unserious," and they, too, take at face value what Austin says about "normal" and "parasitical" (for example, joking) uses of language; they have thought that Austin's enterprise lay specifically in the effort to eliminate the parasites (or the "unserious"), and that their task—the general task of philosophy of language—thus consisted in establishing a series of "rules" or safeguards in order to exclude anomaly and to eliminate the *scandal* of *infelicity*. Thus it is that, working to improve the Austinian "heritage," one of the most famous and currently most fashionable American philosophers, H. P. Grice, has drawn from the performative something that he and his followers call "a logic of conversation." The chief rule of this conversational logic is the one that Grice calls the "cooperative principle":

> Make your conversational contribution such as is required, at the stage at which it occurs, by the accepted purpose or direction of the talk exchange in which you are engaged.[57]

[55]The principal items of European criticism being, as we have seen, Benveniste's essay, the Royaumont proceedings, and the critique of "seriousness" formulated in particular by Jacques Derrida: see Derrida, "Signature Event Context," in *Glyph*, no. 1 (1977), pp. 172–197, and "Limited Inc.," in *Glyph*, no. 2, (1977).

[56]Especially John R. Searle and H. P. Grice. For Searle, see in particular *Speech Acts: An Essay in the Philosophy of Language* (Cambridge: Cambridge University Press, 1969), and "What Is a Speech Act?" in Max Black, ed., *Philosophy in America* (Ithaca: Cornell University Press, 1965). For Grice, see "Meaning," in *Philosophical Review*, 66 (1957); "Utterer's Meaning, Sentence-Meaning and Word-Meaning," in *Foundations of Language*, 14 (1968); "Utterer's Meaning and Intentions," in *Philosophical Review*, 68 (1959). In 1967–1968, Grice gave a series of lectures at Harvard entitled "Logic and Conversation"; the typescript of these lectures was circulated and had a great influence on the work of many Anglo-Saxon linguists and philosophers. The most famous chapter from these lectures has been published as "Logic and Conversation," in *Speech Acts, Syntax and Semantics*, ed. Peter Cole and Jerry L. Morgan, vol. 3 (New York: Academic Press, 1975).

[57]"Logic and Conversation," in *Speech Acts, Syntax and Semantics*, p. 45.

The subordinate rules, called "maxims," are the following:

[Maxims of quantity]
    1. Make your contribution as informative as is required (for the current purposes of the exchange).
    2. Do not make your contribution more informative than is required.

[Maxims of quality]
    Supermaxim—'Try to make your contribution one that is true.'
    1. Do not say what you believe to be false.
    2. Do not say that for which you lack adequate evidence.

[Maxim of relation]: 'Be relevant.'

[Maxims of manner]
    Supermaxim—'Be perspicuous.'
    1. Avoid obscurity of expression.
    2. Avoid ambiguity.
    3. Be brief (avoid unnecessary prolixity).
    4. Be orderly.[58]

Thus Grice's theory constitutes, in a way, an enterprise aimed at *"correcting"* the possible *unhappinesses* of the performative, an effort to eliminate the scandal of the act of failing inherent in the performative. If, then, on the one hand, critics of "seriousness" reproach Austin for being *too serious*, for his excessive adherence to what is supposedly "normal," Grice's doctrine takes him to task on the other

[58]Ibid, pp. 45–46. This code of course does not sum up Grice's *entire* theory, the essential part of which consists in the logical analysis of rule *violations*, and in what Grice calls *conversational implicatures*. The capacity to recognize "maxims" or ground rules constitutes an important part of the "communicative competence" of each speaker. Any violation of these rules will thus be linguistically aberrant, or "marked," or, literally, "remarkable." This means that such a violation will lead the competent listener to draw a certain number of conclusions, or "conversational implicatures" (irony, for example, is a "conversational implicature" with respect to a specific mode of rule exploitation). In other words, the violations that generate "conversational implicature" have to be noted by the listener precisely *as violations* of maxims, in order for the listener to grasp the logically adequate and necessary "implicatures" (or implications).

hand, implicitly at least, for his excessive adherence to the scandal of the "abnormal" or of infelicity. Hence Grice's effort to correct the abnormal by his own attempt to *normalize* the acts of language—or of the speaking body. By improving the manual—which he takes at face value— Grice, it seems, thinks he has really understood *"how to do things with words."*

Austin has said:

> It's not things, it's philosophers that are simple. You will have heard it said, I expect, that over-simplification is the occupational disease of philosophers, and in a way one might agree with that. But for a sneaking suspicion that it's their occupation. [*PP*, p. 252]

Another American attempt at *correcting* Austin's "unseriousness" is that of Jerrold Katz,[59] in a chapter entitled "How to Save Austin from Austin":

> In this concluding section, we survey a range of cases that have been problems or counter-examples for other accounts of performativeness. In particular, some led Austin to abandon the performative/constative distinction in its original form. We shall try to show that a theory such as the one developed above has no trouble with them. [P. 177]

Thus Katz is attempting, like Benveniste, to reestablish the constative/performative opposition in its "original" purity, and thus to get rid of what Austinian theory finally includes that is "troubling" or "problematic" ("a theory such as the one developed above has *no trouble . . .*"). The solution proposed here is in the Chomskyan tradition: the integration of performative theory within the competence/performance distinction. Such an integration makes it possible to elimi-

---

[59]Jerrold J. Katz, *Propositional Structure and Illocutionary Force* (New York: Crowell, 1977). A remark on the jacket flap summarizes Austin's "unseriousness" from the perspective of this book: "Katz argues that speech act theory is not a theory at all, but an assortment of observations about heterogeneous aspects of the performance of speech acts."

nate from the theory the heterogeneity of the *context* by considering the context as "null" or as "ideal"; this allows the *force* of the act to be reduced, once again, to the *meaning* of the act:

> Austin mistakenly thought that [certain] cases were counter-examples simply because he restricted himself to talking about utterances and actions, to performance. . . . The competence-performance distinction provides us with the benefits of idealization. Like the use of idealization in the theory of gases and mechanics, we do not have to state laws in terms of real objects and events—in our case, utterances and the speech acts they perform. Instead, we can state them in terms of their idealized objects and events such as sentence types, their meaning in the language, that is, their meaning in the null context, and context types. . . . Thus, classifying sentences into performatives and constatives can be carried out on the basis of their senses in the language. . . . [Ibid., pp. 184–185]

Thus one saves Austin from Austin by eliminating from the theory his *very consideration of acts* (as opposed to meanings) and his *reference to the reality* of the context; in this way one is *idealizing* precisely the trivial, incongruous materiality of the real, in order to eliminate the "heterogeneous," in order to have a theory that is homogeneous with symmetrical oppositions that leave no residue. Benveniste's aim was also, in fact, simply to eliminate that troubling "confusion between meaning and reference."

How to save Austin from Austin: as always, when it is a question of "saving" (and, what is more, of idealizing), we may assume the presence—felt, denied—of the *devil.*

> Dona Elvira: Have mercy, Don Juan, grant me, as a last favor, that sweet consolation: *do not deny your salvation.* . . . [iv, vi]

In any case, to save Austin is thus to save him from the devil: from the devil that he is—or that he plays—himself.

Now Don Juan is saved from Don Juan only by being killed. Similarly, Austin's remarkable impact on the history of ideas, the very *success* of his theory, constitutes in reality, paradoxically, a *repression* of his discovery. His historical recognition is achieved only through a theoretical misunderstanding (misreading)—through a denegation both of his *act* and of his *humor*. Of the school of Austin's admirers one may say, word for word, what Baudelaire said of love: "In love as in almost all human affairs, a cordial agreement is the result of a misunderstanding. This misunderstanding is pleasure."[60]

Now if the "Austin effect" is, historically, an effect of "pleasure" (an effect of seduction) *and* an effect of misreading or incomprehension, it is because the misunderstanding itself stems from logic—from a preeminently performative logic. The act carried out by Austin, whatever it may be, is such that it provokes both a great power of impression—and a denegation compulsion. The act accomplished by Austin, in other words, is such that it provokes precisely *an act*— but an act of a special nature. If the linguistic philosophies of Searle, Grice, or Katz, for example, are perlocutory effects of Austin's philosophy, this series of "influences," or of linked effects, is not for all that a constative, cognitive series (that *represents* its referent, which cognitively "reflects" its cause), but a performative series (that refers to its cause only in the very act of *missing* it). The history of ideas is thus a chain of acts that is, at the same time, a chain of errors. The Austin effect, historically an effect of seduction, is necessarily, as such, at the same time, an effect of error.

> Mistake will not in general make an act *void**, though it may make it *excusable*. [*HT*, p. 42; *Austin's emphasis]

If the error is "excusable," it is because this error arises, in fact, from the logic of acts.

---

[60]"Mon coeur mis à nu," in *Oeuvres complètes*, ed. Claude Pichois (Paris: Gallimard, Coll. Bibliothèque de la Pléiade, 1961), pp. 1289–1290.

Austin's theoretical consecration, the institutionalization of his theory of speech acts—an effect of its subversive seduction—is thus achieved only through the loss of its cutting edge, that is, of the subversive aspect of seduction. If Austin, like Don Juan, professes the performative breach, a radical break insofar as it is inherent in the speaking body,[61] the victims of Austinian seduction, like Don Juan's, still do not understand this breach as fundamental or radical, but rather as circumstantial, thus as subject to elimination, essentially correctible. The misunderstanding of seduction, here as in Don Juan's case, occurs because seduction produces an effect of belief. The history of ideas—seduced—believes in the "truth" taught by the master ("a stern master," said Freud, with regard to the humor of the superego), believes thus in the theory, not as a promise, but as an accomplishment, not as desire, but as satisfaction: "How to do things with words," or the manual taken at its word; Don Juan without the cutting edge, the performative without the performance—without force, but full of "meaning."

*

Thus the impact of the performative constitutes, in history, something like a *scientific epidemic*. A "scientific epidemic," according to Lacan, occurs "when something is taken as a simple emergence, whereas it is in fact a radical break" ("Le Symptôme," p. 31).

An epidemic: Freud, too, used to say, as he came to introduce psychoanalysis to America: "They don't know that I am bringing the plague." In fact, the history of psychoanalysis resembles that of the performative, in the sense that, there too, the radical break *took*, became institutionalized, only to be itself repressed, denied, mistaken for a "simple emergence."

What is not understood, what—here as elsewhere—histo-

---

[61]Cf. above, "The Teaching of Rupture" and "The Donjuanian Cutting Edge."

ry is determined not to retain, determined to *miss*, that is, *to refuse in the very gesture of accepting,* is always the radical value—the value of both subversive and self-subversive non-return—with which the original thinker invested the force of *negativity* itself. In the simplifications that followed, historically, the negative has always been understood as what is reducible, what is to be eliminated, that is, as what by definition is opposed, is referred, is *subordinated* to the "normal" or to the "positive." The logic of acts thus becomes, for Grice, a *normative* logic of conversation; Nietzschean negativity is historically recuperated by the attempt at normative "correction" that constituted Nazism; the historical flourishing of psychoanalysis in America incorporated Freudian "repression" as the corrective or normalizing counterpart of *"défoulement,"* of sexual "liberation," and of the "reinforcement of the ego"; similarly, it has been understood, in France and elsewhere, on the basis of Lacan's theory, that the "specular" is to be eliminated, that the term "imaginary" is above all a *pejorative* term, subordinated to the "positive" that is constituted here by the antithesis of the "real" or of the "symbolic." But this is not the case. "You've always been left with the impression," said Lacan in a seminar,

> that progress, the forward step, was to have marked the crushing importance of the "symbolic," with respect to that poor "imaginary" with which I began, by shooting a bullet at it under the pretext of narcissism. Only, imagine the image of the mirror—imagine that its reversal is entirely *real.* . . .

> It is not like a scansion that goes from the best to the worst—from the real to the imaginary, passing through the symbolic, but to take things by wedging.

> The imaginary is a dit-mension as important as the others.

> The imaginary thus is not to be placed in any rank whatsoever.[62]

[62]Unpublished lecture, 13 November 1973.

Now in all these theories (psychoanalysis, the performative, Nietzschean philosophy), radical negativity, as the original thinker understood, discovered it, can*not* be reduced to a negative that is the simple—symmetrical—contrary of the "positive," to a reducible negative, caught up in a normative system. When Austin, for example, refers to the normal/abnormal opposition (a reference for which the critics of "seriousness" reproach him), it is not in order to leave this opposition intact nor to promote the criterion of "normality," but rather—like Freud—in order to analyze the abnormal insofar as it is *constitutive of the normal,* that is, in order to undo or to explode the very criterion of "normality":

> To examine excuses is to examine cases where there has been some abnormality or failure: and as so often, the abnormal will throw light on the normal, will help us to *penetrate the blinding veil of ease and obviousness* that hides the mechanisms of the natural successful act. [*PP,* pp. 179–180]

The "abnormal" here does not take the "normal" as a positive term of reference; on the contrary, it is the "normal" that, in order to be understood, necessarily refers to the "abnormal" that breaches it from within, displaces, corrodes, *unmasks* it: the "normal" is henceforth no longer anything but "the *blinding* veil of comfort and of [the false] evidence" that has to be "penetrated," torn apart by the radical force of the negative.[63]

Now if the Austinian negative does not aim simply to treat the negative as a function of the positive, neither does it aim—it aims still less—simply to reduce the positive to the negative. Even though the term "positive" is in the last analysis undone, the defeat of the positive does not involve

[63]As in psychoanalysis, the negative is thus at once what *resists* understanding and what *opens* the space of interpretation. "If there were no account of slips or misfires, there would be no interpretation," says Lacan ("Le Symptôme," *Scilicet,* no. 6/7, p. 13). And Austin (*Philosophical Papers,* p. 271): "The . . . project of . . . clarifying all possible ways and varieties of *not exactly doing things** . . . has to be carried through if we are ever to understand properly what doing things is" (*Austin's emphasis).

any nihilistic complacency, in particular does not include any teleology of "negation for itself." Paradoxically, radical negativity or the defeat of the positive does not, in Austin, exclude positivism:

> Definition, I would add, explanatory definition, should stand high among our aims: it is not enough to show how clever we are by showing how obscure everything is. Clarity, too, I know, has been said to be not enough; but perhaps it will be time to go into that when we are within measurable distance of achieving clarity on some matter. [*PP*, p. 189]

> I think we should not despair too easily and talk, as people are apt to do, about the *infinite** uses of language. Philosophers will do this when they have listed as many, let us say, as seventeen; but even if there were something like ten thousand uses of language, surely we could list them all in time. [*PP*, p. 234; *Austin's emphasis]

"For the sake of folly," says Nietzsche, "wisdom is mixed in all things. A little wisdom is indeed possible."[64] If negativity resides, in Don Juan's case, in the *lack of satisfaction,* Don Juan, in fact, is *never* satisfied, not even—especially not—with negation. If the devil, in other words, refuses above all to play God, it is especially not in order to *believe* in negativity. The "fallible" is not itself infallible: in a world that is fundamentally without guarantees, one cannot be sure of anything at all, not even of infelicity. In a theater of radically diabolical performances, one cannot really count on anything, not even—especially not—on the act of failing.

> We are often right to say we *know* even in cases where we turn out subsequently to have been mistaken—and indeed we seem always, or practically always, liable to be mistaken. . . . The human intellect and senses are, indeed, *inherently** fallible and delusive, but not by any means *inveterately** so. Machines are inherently liable to break down,

---

[64]*Thus Spake Zarathustra*, trans. Thomas Common (London: George Allen & Unwin Ltd., 6th ed., 1932 [1967]), p. 214.

but good machines don't (often). [*PP*, p. 98; *Austin's emphasis]

Thus radical negativity is not simply "negative"; it is—in a very complex way—positive, it is fecund, it is affirmative. "Non-dupes err" is not, after all a negation, but an affirmation: "One must be a dupe. Dupe, that is, stuck to structure."[65] "Into all abysses do I then carry the Yea-saying of my blessing," says Nietzsche's Zarathustra, "the advocate of living, the advocate of suffering" (p. 213). And Austin, in turn:

> In philosophy, there are many mistakes that it is no disgrace to have made: to make a first-water, ground-floor mistake, so far from being easy, takes one (*one*) form of philosophical genius. [*PP*, p. 203; Austin's emphasis]

> A disagreement as to what we should say is not to be shied off, but to be pounced upon: for the explanation of it can hardly fail to be illuminating. If we light on an electron that rotates the wrong way, that is a discovery, a portent to be followed up, not a reason for chucking physics: and by the same token, a genuinely loose or eccentric talker is a rare specimen to be prized. [*PP*, p. 184]

Thus negativity, fundamentally fecund and affirmative, and yet without positive reference, is above all *that which escapes the negative/positive alternative.*

> A belief in opposites and dichotomies encourages, among other things, a blindness to the combinations and dissociations of adverbs that are possible, even to such obvious facts that we can act at once on impulse and intentionally.

> 'Voluntarily' and 'involuntarily,' then, are not opposed in the obvious sort of way that they are made to be in philosophy or jurisprudence.

---

[65]Jacques Lacan, unpublished lecture, 13 November 1973.

In general, it will pay us to take nothing for granted or as obvious about negations and opposites. It does not pay to assume that a word must have an opposite, or one opposite, whether it is a 'positive' word like 'wilfully,' or a 'negative' word like 'inadvertently.' [*PP*, pp. 195, 191–192]

"Saying unveils itself," says Lacan likewise, "in escaping the said":

Henceforth it assures this privilege only by formulating itself as "saying no," if, in going toward meaning, it is the holding back [contien] that one grasps there, not the contradiction—the response, not the repetition in negation—the refusal, not the correction. ["L'Etourdit," p. 9]

Radical negativity (or "saying no") belongs neither to *negation*, nor to *opposition*, nor to *correction* ("normalization"), nor to *contradiction* (of the positive and the negative, the normal and the abnormal, the "serious" and the "unserious," "clarity" and "obscurity")—it belongs precisely to *scandal*: to the scandal of their nonopposition. This scandal of the *outside of the alternative*, of a negativity that is neither negative nor positive, is the one that is summarized, in Kierkegaard, the philosopher-seducer, in a style that could hardly be more Donjuanian (or Austinian, or Lacanian):

If you marry, you will regret it; if you do not marry, you will also regret it . . . ; whether you marry or do not marry, you will regret both. Laugh at the world's follies, you will regret it; weep over them, you will also regret that . . . ; whether you laugh at the world's follies or weep over them, you will regret both. . . . Hang yourself, you will regret it; do not hang yourself, you will also regret that . . . ; whether you hang yourself or do not hang yourself, you will regret both. This, Gentlemen, is the sum and substance of all philosophy. [*Either/Or*, p. 37]

Now it is just this scandal of unclassifiable radicality, of a force whose negativity is such that it splinters the very structure of the negative/positive alternative, that history cannot assimilate. History demands that Don Juan declare himself: that he marry *or* not marry; that he choose life *or* death. "And also from thee they want Yea or Nay," Nietzsche writes. "Alas! thou wouldst set thy chair betwixt For and Against?" (*Zarathustra*, p. 107). Similarly, the history of ideas wants Austin to declare himself: is he *serious*, or is he *not serious*? Is he trying to *clarify*, or to *obscure* the distinction between constative and performative? Let him come down on one side or the other: is he a linguist, *or* is he a philosopher?[66] That Austin may be *both* philosopher *and* linguist, and at the same time, properly speaking, quite *outside the alternative—neither* philosopher *nor* linguist (just as a psychoanalyst is *neither* a psychiatrist *nor* a psychologist)—this can scarcely satisfy the history of ideas, which in fact reproaches Austin for being too much a linguist for philosophy (at Royaumont), and at the same time too philosophical for linguistics (Benveniste: cf. pp. 231–232 and 238). What history always misunderstands, fails to recognize, or fails—actively—to retain, is the negative beyond the alternative, or radical negativity.

Now radical negativity is what constitutes in fact the *analytic* or *performative* dimension of a thought: at once what *makes it an act*, and what makes for its *humor*. (Parallel to Austinian humor, one can find a Nietzschean humor, and a Lacanian humor; here again, they have been little noted by the history of theory—of "ideas.") *What history cannot assimilate is thus the implicitly analytical dimension of all radical or fecund thoughts*, of all new theories: the "force" of their "performance" (always somewhere subversive) and their "residual smile" (always somewhere self-subversive).

---

[66]This is the question that keeps coming up in the Royaumont discussions. Cf. Austin's response: "I shall not attempt to give a response so far as the boundary between linguistics and analytic philosophy is concerned, whatever one may understand by that. I shall simply say, by way of *warning*, if you like, that I for one do not think that the frontier is as clear-cut as Professor Ayer seemed to imply" (*CR*, pp. 347–348).

Paradoxically, what history, as a general rule, fails to recognize, or denies, in a new theory of whatever sort—*owing to the historical success of the theory itself*—is nothing but that which has *made history*, precisely, of the theory.

What we have grasped, deciphered, or analyzed in connection with Austin's theory and the misunderstandings of its history thus has a general validity in terms of the functioning of the history of ideas as such, proves to be revelatory of the dynamics of the historical *doing* of theory, on the one hand, and on the other of the nonlinear and discontinuous manner in which history *integrates* this doing in the very gesture of repressing its force and denying it. "The true eternity," writes Kierkegaard, "does not lie behind either/or, but before it" (*Either/Or*, p. 38). History only registers theoretical acts or idea-events within the structure—always an ideological structure—of opposition or alternatives, but it is precisely what lies outside the alternative that makes an event, that makes an act, that makes history. Paradoxically, the things that have no history (like humor) are what make history. The self-referentiality of history is, in other words, itself condemned to "misfire": but this constative misfiring is what *makes* history, is indeed what the historical performative derives from. History does not include, either, any true "knowledge": its only knowledge is the *savoir-faire* of its own misunderstanding. (This is applicable, no doubt, at once to History, to the history of ideas, and to the history of theories which is always only, in the last analysis, the history of institutions: "History of psychoanalysis," and so on.)

There exists, then a relationship between what Austin *does* and what, in history, is misunderstood about his thesis, or what is misconstrued from his saying (doing): the same type of relation—of misunderstanding that is somehow logical or a qualitative leap—as the one that exists, on the other hand, in the myth, between what Don Juan *does* and his *effect* on others. If myth is, in general, an allegory of history, the Don Juan myth may become, specifically, an allegory of the way in which history at once *makes* itself and gives itself to be *misunderstood*: an allegory of the stone banquet. If the *stone* of the feast is in reality what history cannot assimilate—what is indigestible in the language feast (Austinian, Lacanian, Freudian, Nietzschean language)—it is also, at the same time, the very stone that makes—or builds—history, the stone that, although unassimilated, is nevertheless the *cornerstone* of History.

A New Type of Materialism, or the Gift of What One Does Not Have

At the beginning of this section, I said that I would try to say what Austin *does* with words. I have just suggested that he not only produces laughter, produces pleasure, produces slips and stumbles, explodes beliefs and prejudices, produces a theoretical fiasco or *fails* to meet his own ends, to keep his own promise, but also that, in doing this (like Freud, like Lacan, like Nietzsche, and moreover like Marx), he *makes history*: that his speech act participates in what one might well call the *logic of the scandal* of historical practice, owing to the very fact that it has enough force to set in motion a systematic series of misunderstandings, that is, a historical operation—no doubt unconscious—of repression.

Let me go further: if Austin (like Freud, like Lacan, like Nietzsche, like Marx) indeed makes history, he does so above all else as a thinker with a new conception of the act and of the referent, by displacing *historical knowledge,* and thus modifying the conception of history itself.

Marx, too, was wont to say that from the way history misunderstood itself stemmed the performance of revolutions—or historical practice. Granting primordial value to work, he too stressed the inherent value of "doing"—of "production," that is, both of the act and of its referential effect of modifying reality. Like Austin, although from a different point of view and in an entirely different context,

145

Marx was above all preoccupied with the radical schism between "force" and "meaning": it is precisely this schism that he christened "ideology."[67] Marx, in other words, like Austin, was preoccupied with the *disparity* between "saying" and "doing"—insofar as this disparity is constitutive of the ambiguous, problematic, contradictory truth of the *social speaking body*. Austin and Marx are thus both materialists of the speaking body.

In Austin's case, however, it is no longer, as with Marx, a reference to the *economy* that materialism exploits, but a reference to the physical.[68] Reference to the physical is, moreover, traditional within the general trend of "analytic philosophy," perhaps under the (distant) influence of its founder, Bertand Russell, whose method of "logical atomism"—inspired by physical analysis—constituted one of the earliest models of the philosophical enterprise that the history of ideas has come to call, in fact, "analysis" (in the English sense of the term).[69]

> Let us consider further the example of physics for a moment. You find, if you read the works of physicists, that they reduce matter down to certain elements—atoms, ions, corpuscles, or what not. But in any case the sort of thing that you are aiming at in the physical analysis of matter is to get down to the very little bits of matter that are still just like matter in the fact that they persist through time, and that they travel about in space. They have in fact all the ordinary everyday properties of physical matter, not the matter that one has in everyday life—they do not taste or smell or appear to the naked eye—but they have the properties that you very soon get to when you travel toward physics from ordinary life. Things of that sort, I say, are not the ultimate constituents of matter in any metaphysical sense. Those things are . . . logical fictions. . . .[70]

[67]Another term that has made a place for itself but whose historical *fortune* is in fact just as ambiguous as that of the "performative."

[68]See for example the *Cahiers de Royaumont*, pp. 338, 349, 350; and *Philosophical Papers*, p. 184.

[69]See above, n. 24.

[70]Bertrand Russell, "What There Is" (excerpt from "The Philosophy of

In fact, the model of contemporary physics is doubtless the most apt to account for both the specificity and the originality of Austinian materialism. What Austin analyzes are in a way the "atoms" of language, that is, "very little bits of matter" of language,[71] "that are still just like matter in the fact that they persist through time, and that they travel about in space."[72] No doubt, in the eyes of a simplistic or traditional materialism, the very concept of the "matter of language" would itself be susceptible to the charge of "idealism"—based on a "contradiction in terms." But it is precisely here that Austin's originality lies, for through the new concept of "language *act*" he explodes both the opposition and the separation between matter (or body) and language: matter, like the act, *without being reducible to language*, is no longer entirely *separable* from it, either.

The traditional antithesis—materialism/idealism—subordinated to the metaphysical separation between body and language, is thus itself, here, suspended or undone, being a part in turn, once again, of the structure of the alternative or of the metaphysics of "things," that is, of the *traditional* physics of matter. But contemporary physics, atomic and relativist, has in fact demonstrated that the unity of "matter in itself" is from now on an outdated concept, that matter exists not in itself but as a *relation* to *energy*, all loss of matter forming, by that very token, an enormous recrudescence of energy. Matter, in modern physics, thus no longer

---

Logical Atomism"), in R. R. Ammerman, ed., *Classics of Analytic Philosophy*, p. 27.

[71]Cf. Austin, *Cahiers de Royaumont*, p. 332: "We begin by drawing up a list of everything in language that has to do with the subject we are examining: all the words we might use, all the expressions in which these words might appear. . . . We are careful, too, to take up a problem that bears upon a sufficiently *limited* point. For me, that is the main thing: a complete and *painstaking* inventory of everything connected with the subject under investigation; and the choice of a *limited* subject, at the outset."

[72]Cf. Austin, *Cahiers de Royaumont*, p. 335: "*If a language has lasted* on the lips and the pens of civilized men, if it has been capable of serving in all circumstances of life *through the ages*, it is probable that the distinctions it marks, like the connections it makes, in its multiple turns of phrase, are not entirely without value."

has *absolute* existence, but only a *relative* existence within an interaction of *matter/energy relations*.

I suggest that it is in a sense parallel to the discovery of the matter/energy unity that Austin discovers the singular "unity" of the speech act, that is, a relation, precisely, between the matter of language (little bits of sentences, phrases, signifiers, atoms of the speaking body) and energy or (illocutionary) "force," that space of undecidability between matter and energy, between "things" and "events." And here again, energy is obtained only by the explosion of semantic atoms, the recrudescence of force is achieved only at the price of the loss or the bursting of the signifying matter.

Thus we are dealing, in the Austinian discovery (as, moreover, in the Freudian discovery), with the intuition of nothing less than a *new type of materialism.* I suggest that Austin's materialism lies *between* the materialism of psychoanalysis and that of atomic physics, since, like psychoanalysis, it is concerned with the speaking body, and since it displaces the notion of act in the same way that the physics of relativity displaces that of matter.

In fact, like every thought of desire, of force and explosion, Austinian materialism is a materialism of the *residue,* that is, literally, of the *trivial*: a materialism of the speaking body, and one whose matter—matter for scandal—is nothing other than the *feast stone*—as cornerstone of History.

*

If the matter of History is made up, among other things, of speech acts it is because for Austin, as for Einstein, matter itself has ceased, above all, to be a "thing": *matter itself is an event.* According to this new type of materialism, history no longer proceeds so much, as it did for Marx, from a logic of *contradiction* (of contradictions between classes or contradictions inherent in the discourse of the dominant class), but rather from a logic of *scandal*. In fact, if the category of contradiction is subordinated to the logic of identity—that is, still and always, to the structure of the alternative—scandal is precisely what causes that structure to break up. Scandal, as Austin suggests "in passing," in one of his offhand remarks, is linked to the criterion of "infelicity" and thus requires, to be understood, a philosophy of the performative, whereas contradiction, on the other hand, has the disadvantage of being understandable only within a logic that is still exclusively constative.

> I refer to the discovery that the ways we can do wrong, speak outrageously, in uttering conjunctions of 'factual' statements, are more numerous than merely by contradiction. . . .

> There is a common feeling of outrage in all these cases. But we must not use some blanket term, . . . 'contradiction,' because there are very great differences. There are more ways of killing a cat than drowning it in butter; but this is the sort of thing (as the proverb indicates) we overlook: *there are more ways of outraging speech than contradiction merely.* The major questions are: how many ways, and why they outrage speech, and wherein the outrage lies?

> In conclusion, we see that in order to explain what can go wrong with statements we cannot just concentrate on the proposition involved . . . as has been done traditionally. We must consider the total situation . . . the total speech act. . . . So the *total speech act* in the total speech situation is *emerging from logic piecemeal.* . . .

> One of the things that has been happening lately in philosophy is that close attention has been given even 'statements' which, though not false exactly nor yet 'contradictory,' are yet *outrageous.* For instance, statements which refer to something which does not exist as, for example, 'The present King of France is bald.' *There might be a temptation to assimilate this to purporting to bequeath something which you do not own.* [HT, pp. 47, 48, 52, 20]

The scandal, according to Austin, thus arises from the performative logic of "giving what you don't have," through which, moreover, Lacan in fact defines love (*Ecrits*, p. 69).

The scandal, in other words, is always in a certain way the scandal of the promise of love, the scandal of the *untenable,* that is, still and always, the scandal—Donjuanian in the extreme—of the promising animal, incapable of keeping his promise, incapable of not making it, powerless both to fulfill the commitment and to avoid *committing* himself—to avoid playing beyond his means, playing, indeed, the devil: the scandal of the speaking body, who in failing himself and others makes an act of that failure, and makes history.

Thus Austin, like Lacan, like Nietzsche, like others still, instigators of the historical scandal, Don Juans of History, are in reality *bequeathing* us what they do not have: their *word,* their authority, their promise.

Enjoyers of language, spillers of ink, Sisyphuses of the banquet stone, theoretical seducers, the Don Juans of History *flirt* with shades, *invite* the statue, seek above all to *make* the banquet stone talk:

> Parla dunque! Che chiedi? Che vuoi?
>
> . . .
>
> Parla, parla, ascoltando ti sto.[73]

Thinkers of desire, of force, of radical negativity, they do not *believe* in the promising animal, but, blasé, they continue nevertheless to desire, to promise, to commit their naïveté.

Modern Don Juans, they know that *truth is only an act.* That is why they subvert truth and do not promise it, but *promise themselves to it.* Never considering their own answers to be satisfying, they remain the scandalous authors of the infelicity that never ceases to make history.

---

[73]"Speak then! What are you asking for? What do you want? . . . Speak, speak, for I am listening to you" (Don Giovanni to the statue, in Mozart's opera).

Library of Congress Cataloging in Publication Data

Felman, Shoshana.
   The literary speech act.

   Translation of: Le scandale du corps parlant.
   Includes bibliographical references.
   1. Speech   acts   (Linquistics)   2. Performative   (Philoso-
phy)   3. Molière, 1622–1673. Dom Juan.   4. Austin, J. L. (John
Langshaw), 1911–1960.   I. Title.
P95.55.F413   1983   401   83-45144
ISBN 0-8014-1458-X (alk. paper)